College Teaching and Learning: Preparing for New Commitments

Robert E. Young, Kenneth E. Eble, *Editors*

NEW DIRECTIONS FOR TEACHING AND LEARNING

ROBERT E. YOUNG, *Editor-in-Chief*
University of Wisconsin

KENNETH E. EBLE, *Consulting Editor*
University of Utah, Salt Lake City

Number 33, Spring 1988

Paperback sourcebooks in
The Jossey-Bass Higher Education Series

Jossey-Bass Inc., Publishers
San Francisco • London

Robert E. Young, Kenneth E. Eble (eds.).
College Teaching and Learning: Preparing for New Commitments.
New Directions for Teaching and Learning, no. 33.
San Francisco: Jossey-Bass, Spring 1988.

New Directions for Teaching and Learning
Robert E. Young, *Editor-in-Chief*
Kenneth E. Eble, *Consulting Editor*

Copyright © 1988 by Jossey-Bass Inc., Publishers
and
Jossey-Bass Limited

New Directions for Teaching and Learning is published quarterly
by Jossey-Bass Inc., Publishers, 350 Sansome Street, San Francisco,
California, 94104. Application to mail at second-class postage rates
is pending at San Francisco, California, and at additional mailing
offices. POSTMASTER: Send address changes to *New Directions for
Teaching and Learning,* Jossey-Bass Inc., Publishers, 350 Sansome
Street, San Francisco, California 94104.

Editorial correspondence should be sent to the Editor-in-Chief,
Robert E. Young, Dean, University of Wisconsin Center, Fox Valley,
1478 Midway Rd., Menasha, Wisconsin 54952.

Library of Congress Catalog Card Number LC 85-644763

International Standard Serial Number ISSN 0271-0633

International Standard Book Number ISBN 1-55542-928-9

Cover art by WILLI BAUM

Manufactured in the United States of America

Ordering Information

$3\,78.125$
$C\,697$

The paperback sourcebooks listed below are published quarterly and can be ordered either by subscription or single copy.

Subscriptions cost $48.00 per year for institutions, agencies, and libraries. Individuals can subscribe at the special rate of $36.00 per year *if payment is by personal check.* (Note that the full rate of $48.00 applies if payment is by institutional check, even if the subscription is designated for an individual.) Standing orders are accepted.

Single copies are available at $11.95 when payment accompanies order. (California, New Jersey, New York, and Washington, D.C., residents please include appropriate sales tax.) For billed orders, cost per copy is $11.95 plus postage and handling.

Substantial discounts are offered to organizations and individuals wishing to purchase bulk quantities of Jossey-Bass sourcebooks. Please inquire.

Please note that these prices are for the academic year 1987–88 and are subject to change without notice. Also, some titles may be out of print and therefore not available for sale.

To ensure correct and prompt delivery, all orders must give either the *name of an individual* or an *official purchase order number.* Please submit your order as follows:

Subscriptions: specify series and year subscription is to begin.
Single Copies: specify sourcebook code (such as, TL1) and first two words of title.

Mail orders for United States and Possessions, Latin America, Canada, Japan, Australia, and New Zealand to:
Jossey-Bass Inc., Publishers
350 Sansome Street
San Francisco, California 94104

Mail orders for all other parts of the world to:
Jossey-Bass Limited
28 Banner Street
London EC1Y 8QE

New Directions for Teaching and Learning Series
Robert E. Young, *Editor-in-Chief*
Kenneth E. Eble, *Consulting Editor*

Contents

Editor's Notes

New Directions for Teaching and Learning (NDTL) is now thirty-two volumes *"old."* Kenneth E. Eble, first with John F. Noonan and then alone, has edited this series since its inception in 1980. With this volume, I succeed Eble as editor-in-chief. To mark this transition of editorial leadership, we have produced a volume that both looks backwards on the series and ahead to the future shape of NDTL. More important, the volume takes stock of where college teaching and learning find themselves as we approach the last decade of the twentieth century.

The idea of the volume was to invite a select group of previous NDTL editors to write about the developments since their volumes were published. In just 100 pages we hoped to provide an interesting and useful view of what is new and important in a number of key areas of college teaching and learning. As the volume developed we think that we have succeeded in offering both a fresh analysis of the recent past in these areas and challenging ideas for the future.

We also learned again about the great diversity and changing nature of the research and writing about college learning and teaching. The chapters in this volume offer a range of approaches and styles, reflective both of the NDTL series and the general literature on college teaching and learning. This range, we believe, is a great strength. College teaching and learning, like few other topics, benefits as much from hard-nosed research reports and reviews as from searching essays and critiques.

We learned that in the field of college teaching and learning, as in any field, there is a succession of spokespersons. We invited former NDTL editors to write about the topic of their particular volumes, this many years hence. In most cases that is what the chapters represent. Two chapters are notable exceptions. First, Peter Seldin, though a previous NDTL editor, did not prepare the first volume on the evaluation of teaching. That was ably done by Grace French-Lazovik. Seldin, however, has become the acknowledged leader in this area with his work over the past several years and has thus prepared the chapter on evaluating college teaching. Then, Paul R. Pintrich makes his first contribution to NDTL in this volume. When we approached Bill McKeachie to write the chapter on student learning, he right away suggested that his associate, Pintrich, was doing the best work in the field at this time. Pintrich is very much of a new generation of contributors to college teaching and learning, so we thought it apt to include him in a volume that looks to the future as well as to the past.

1

Not all the topics relevant to college teaching and learning could be covered in this short volume. We have tried to select topics and authors that raised considerable interest in previous volumes. We tried to choose issues that were currently alive in the coffee room conversations of college and university faculty members as well as in the national conferences. A scheme for the future of NDTL is described below, and we have tried to foreshadow in this volume the kind of topics that the series will consider in the future.

Future Shape of NDTL

This volume provides a new editor an opportunity to introduce a new approach to structuring the series. College teaching and learning constitutes a wide domain, one that has a lot of territories. The words *learning* and *teaching* themselves call up distinct activities and different traditions of research and practice. As we have planned for the future of NDTL, we thought it would be useful to define the field, as a guide for future volume editors, authors, and readers.

This series will undertake coverage of eight topic areas in the domain of college-level teaching and learning:

- curriculum
- teaching strategies and techniques
- instructional development
- faculty and faculty development
- students and learning
- administrative support for learning and teaching
- contexts for college teaching and learning
- research on college teaching and learning.

We will try to include a volume in each of these categories every two years. We will use this approach flexibly though. The most important concerns of college teachers might demand that more than one volume be developed in an area during a particular period. For instance, the current interest in pedagogy may mean that a number of NDTL sourcebooks on strategies and techniques will be developed. The categories we have chosen, however, represent enduring interests of college teachers and those who support them. So, a series that sticks close to these topics should be a useful and stimulating one.

As all the Jossey-Bass sourcebook series, NDTL depends on the active involvement of the profession in shaping and producing the series. Topics for NDTL volumes need to come from the field as often as they come from the editor's desk. Let me finish these Editor's Notes by inviting readers of the series to propose topics for future volumes and to contribute to the series as volume editors and authors. The vitality of NDTL over its first eight years has been in the variety of experiences and point-of-view offered by its thirty-nine editors and more than two hundred authors. My hope is that the next thirty-two volumes will be just as lively and just as important in charting the new directions for teaching and learning in American colleges and universities.

Robert E. Young
Editor-in-Chief

Robert E. Young is dean of the University of Wisconsin Center–Fox Valley. He was editor of NDTL no. 3, Fostering Critical Thinking, *and has been an author of sourcebooks and an editorial consultant to Jossey-Bass since that time. With this volume he begins as editor-in-chief of* New Directions for Teaching and Learning.

Despite the resurgence of the liberal arts, an undergraduate curriculum still requires a synthesis of liberal and practical learning.

Assessing the Prospects for Liberal Learning and Careers

Charles S. Green III, Richard G. Salem

"Driven by careerism and overshadowed by graduate and professional education, many of the nation's colleges and universities are more successful in credentialing than in providing a quality education for their students. . . . Narrow vocationalism, with its emphasis on skills training, dominates the campus" (Boyer, 1987, p. 1). This is the way the Carnegie Foundation characterizes American higher education in 1987. The description can hardly be denied. It is echoed in the enrollments through the 1970s and 1980s (cf. Solmon, 1981) as well as almost all the recent critiques of higher education (cf. Bloom, 1987; Hirsch, 1987; Association of American Colleges, 1985; National Institute of Education, 1984; Bennett, 1984).

Of course, Harvard, Yale, and the College of William and Mary were founded to educate a professional clergy and to support the churches of the colonies. The new colleges that proliferated in the mid eighteenth century had a similar vocational purpose, as did the land-grant colleges founded after the Morrill Act in 1862. Alexis de Tocqueville observed in the 1830s in *Democracy in America:* "The American can devote to general education only the early years of life. At fifteen they enter upon their calling, and thus their education generally ends at the age when ours begins. If it continues beyond that point, it aims only towards a partic-

R. E. Young, K. E. Eble (eds.). *College Teaching and Learning: Preparing for New Commitments.*
New Directions for Teaching and Learning, no. 33. San Francisco: Jossey-Bass, Spring 1988.

ular specialized and profitable purpose; one studies science as one takes up a business; and one takes up only those applications whose immediate practicality is recognized."

As anyone educated in this century knows, this vocational tradition has coexisted with another equally persistent tradition, one emphasizing the virtues of contemplation, of knowledge for its own sake, and demanding that education serve the needs of individual human development. This tradition of liberal education clearly has been the weaker one in America, and its practitioners consequently have been forced to justify it in practical terms. Thomas Jefferson (1984), in his "Bill for the More General Diffusion of Knowledge" before the Virginia General Assembly, argued for liberal education in serving political goals. One of these goals Jefferson proposed was to sensitize the citizenry to its leaders' potential for corruption and tyranny; a liberal education "would . . . illuminate . . . the minds of the people at large, and more especially to give them knowledge of those facts which history exhibiteth, that possessed thereby of the experience of other ages and countries, they may be enabled to know ambition in all its shapes" (p. 365).

Three hundred years of compromises between these two traditions have given rise to the bewildering complexity and diversity of American higher education. Although practical training has been a dominant emphasis throughout American history, the tradition of liberal education has spawned institutions fully and exclusively committed to the liberal arts tradition, such as Saint John's College in Maryland. Moreover, the liberal arts tradition has led a persistent if precarious existence within even the most thoroughly vocational public universities in the form of general education programs. Compromise has seldom been entirely satisfactory, so the history of American higher education can be described also as a succession of both broad reform movements or localized efforts to recreate the undergraduate program. The most intense of these efforts have taken place in the context of national political or economic crisis: the period of rapid economic expansion following the Civil War; massive migration from Europe and Asia; World War I; the Great Depression; World War II; the Cold War and the challenge of Sputnik; the Civil Rights and Vietnam War crises; and, currently, the Japanese economic challenge of the late 1970s and 1980s. This should not be surprising since both the traditions of vocationalism and liberalism have justification in terms of specific national political and economic goals (Litt, 1981).

It was this history, these traditions, and their shifting compromise that provided the context for *Liberal Learning and Careers* (Green and Salem, 1981). Not surprising, this same ebb and flow of the American college curriculum makes a look seven years later a useful task. Where does the tide now lay between liberal education and career preparation? The 1981 sourcebook had two purposes. The first was to trace the reasons for the massive enrollment shift during the 1970s from the liberal arts to such vocational programs as engineering, social welfare, health services, business administration, and criminal justice. The second purpose was to assess the kinds of responses that the liberal arts could and should take to enrollment shifts. This present chapter, some 300,000 college degrees and twenty-seven volumes of *New Directions of Teaching and Learning* later, picks up these enrollment trends and curricular responses a half decade later, evaluates the current relationship between careers and liberal learning, and projects this great historic compromise into the future.

Subsequent Developments

There was a unifying theme to be found in our 1981 volume, though this theme has become clearer to us only after some six years of further thought on the topic and in the context of more recent scholarship. Our authors agreed that the controversy between a tradition stressing knowledge for its own sake and a tradition stressing practical training is a fruitless one. It is fruitless because the controversy assumes that the traditions are polar opposites, that we must choose between traditions, and that one tradition has clear-cut and demonstrable advantages over the other. Instead, the two traditions, we believed then, should be viewed as tendencies or forces that are both linked and opposed. Indeed, this conception of linked and opposite tendencies pervades social thought from antiquity to the present: "From Empedocles' view of the world divided by love and hate to Freud's theory of death and eros, from the medieval idea of a universal determinism coupled with individual freedom to Marx' view of men as partly free and partly involuntary political actors under given historical circumstances, from the Confucian concepts of Ying and Yang to Kant's ideas of 'unsocial sociability': the variations increase but the theme remains" (Bendix and Berger, 1959, p. 95; for a related view of the paradoxical quality of education, see Brann, 1979).

This conception leads us to expect that any education that emphasizes knowledge for its own sake without also attending to the practical implications of that knowledge is irrelevant, if not sterile. Similarly, practical training devoid of any attention to the concerns of liberal learning (esthetics, history, ethics, and so on) is likely to be used mechanically, without an informed consideration of its limits, and so is doomed to eventual failure even if not harm.

The Limits of Practical Training

The limitations of practical training are important to articulate: Purely vocational training overlooks the potential practicality of knowledge for its own sake. It is woefully narrow in its focus on "can do" rather than "why do?" It is shortsighted in its stress on the immediate relevance and applicability of knowledge. And, in its focus on the material benefits to be gained by societies and individuals through practical training, it overlooks far more important intangible outcomes of education.

The Practicality of the Impractical. Einstein, it is said, once argued that there is nothing more practical than a good theory. We could review the familiar and frequent examples of the unanticipated and serendipitous ways that basic research in physical and natural sciences, over the pursuit of knowledge for pure amusement, has led to the eradication of hunger and disease, to improved standards of living and, paradoxically, to advances in the technology of war. More relevant for our review, though, are examples of the practicality of "impractical" endeavors in the social sciences and humanities.

In its effort to become competitive on a worldwide scale, American business management has turned to Japan for the secrets of increased productivity. There are several ironies in this development. First, the revered quality circles were devised in the 1950s, based on what the Japanese thought at the time were the most advanced *American* managerial practices. Though participative management was indeed being discussed in the more sophisticated American management circles, such management was rarely practiced by the members of those circles, despite research by American and European sociologists that had for over a decade been establishing the value of participation in the work place (Whyte, 1982; Guest, 1987). Recently, our scholars have begun to analyze why participative management failed to be adopted here until the 1980s, why the particular Japanese approach to participation may not work without considerable modification in the context of American culture, and why other experiments in participative management (for example, worker co-ops in Spain, Yugoslavia's worker councils) might be more appropriate.

Other evidence of the practicality of the impractical is to be found in Clifford Adelman's careful review of *The Standardized Test Scores of College Graduates, 1964–1982* (1986). Adelman reviewed results for twenty-three tests used in selecting applicants for graduate school, including the three most widely used: the Graduate Record Examination (GRE), the Law School Aptitude Test (LSAT), and the Graduate Management Admissions Test (GMAT). After examining a number of background variables (for example, age, gender, race, and social class), he concluded that the only variable that correlated consistently and significantly with test scores was undergraduate major. Specifically, he concluded that: (1) "Undergraduates who major in professional and occupational fields consistently *under perform* those who major in traditional arts and sciences fields (emphasis in the original). (2) Students who major in a field characterized by formal thought, structural relationships, abstract models, symbolic languages, and deductive reasoning consistently out perform others on these examinations. (3) The liberal arts majors who did the best consistently on the GRE, LSAT, and GMAT were philosophy majors!" (p. 35).

Thus, we have recent evidence that undergraduates who major in the humanities have a decided advantage in getting admitted to professional schools over their brethren who majored in more vocational fields.

But what about those who decided to pursue graduate study in the humanities rather than the professions? Are they not doomed to unemployment or at best underemployment as cab drivers and clerks? Another study demonstrates that such conventional wisdom is largely a myth. *Science, Engineering, and Humanities Doctorates in the United States: 1983 Profile* (Maxfield and Belisle, 1985) reports that (1) a large majority of humanities Ph.D.s are employed in academic work; (2) a substantial minority have chosen nonacademic careers, but these are typically in the professions, management, and administration where they are doing well in terms of both financial rewards and the intangible benefits of challenge and autonomy; (3) few are unemployed or working part-time.

The Relevance of Moral Values and Ethics. As we pointed out in the editor's notes for the 1981 sourcebook, having the knowledge to do something practical does not give us the wisdom to know whether, when, and where that thing should be done. This seems increasingly realized in the business world (see Fowler, 1987b; Rohatyn, 1987; Behrman and Levine, 1984; Shad, 1987; Otten, 1986; Stricharchuk, 1986). It is not unusual to hear corporate leaders, not just their critics, say that students "should learn to humanize the corporation rather than corporatize the family or the individual, and they must understand the ethical implications of every management decision they make" (Behrman and Levine, 1984, p. 142).

The Shortsightedness of the Immediately Practical. Even the occupational relevance of an education should not be judged by what it will do for a person in the job market today or in the future. To be sure, a young person who has gotten a bachelor's degree in business with an accounting major may have more job offers and will start out at a higher salary than a person with a liberal arts degree with a major in English, philosophy, or sociology. But what happens in twenty-five years, when the company that accounting major joined is looking for a new chief executive officer? A board of directors will be looking for someone to plan the company's future over the next ten to twenty years. Most likely, they will not choose someone narrowly trained but rather will select someone with a broad understanding of the complex and changing environment for a company in the twenty-first century. That someone is likely to have had a general liberal arts education and to be

- A person with some grounding in the natural and physical

sciences who can understand the implications for the company of new scientific discoveries and inventions

• Someone educated in the social sciences who understands what poverty in Asia, Africa, and Latin America might mean for the company's ability to market its products or services and who understands why people in these poor countries resent the intrusion of American companies into their affairs

• A person with sufficient background in the humanities to articulate (even in a foreign language) the company's policies and objectives to its diverse constituencies: leaders of other countries, workers, union leaders, educators, politicians, and so on

• Someone who has the ethical sensibilities to prevent the company from producing defective or hazardous products, maintaining an unsafe working environment, fixing prices in collusion with other companies, bribing public officials, or otherwise abusing its power

• An individual with sufficient ecological awareness to prohibit the company from adversely affecting its social and biological environment, the esthetic sensitivity to produce products that are beautiful as well as useful, and the ability to create a work environment that is an esthetically pleasurable one.

Recent evidence seems to support this contention. AT&T, in a study of the managerial employees it hired in 1956, found that 43 percent of the employees who majored in the liberal arts reached the highest managerial levels within twenty years after their hiring, whereas just 32 percent of those with business degrees and 23 percent of those with engineering degrees did as well. Moreover, the study revealed that its humanities and social sciences graduates had significantly greater leadership skills, communication skills, creative ability, and breadth of intellectual interest than those who majored in other areas, including business. In addition, their organization, planning, and decision-making skills were found to equal those of business graduates and to be superior to those of all other majors. (A copy of the AT&T study can be obtained for $1 from the Association of American Colleges, 1818 R Street, N.W., Washington, D.C. 20009.)

Unfortunately the long-run payoff of liberal learning is seldom fully appreciated by undergraduates. As Solmon reported in our 1981 book, "in the corporate, government, and military employment sectors, those who have worked longer are more likely to see a link with their majors . . . At the beginning, the relationship question seems to be evaluated according to the degree of *direct* application of course materials, whereas after obtaining work experience, the relationship is viewed in terms of the ability to apply the *broad* set of skills and competencies acquired during the college years" (1981, p. 23). A longitudinal study of the sociology graduates of Bowling Green State University (Jacoby, Pugh,

Snyder, and Spreitzer, 1984) found that similar changes in perception had taken place, a finding replicated by the University of Virginia in its study of the 1971 through 1981 graduates of its College of Arts and Sciences (Kingston and Nock, 1985).

Is Money Everything? The benefits of a liberal education surely go beyond good jobs and high salaries. Even workaholics do more than work: They vote, try to raise their children decently, try to be good spouses, improve themselves through leisure pursuits, worry about and often try to do something about drug abuse, crime, pollution, war, racism and sexism, and poverty. A liberal arts education does not guarantee happiness, but it can give persons the knowledge and sensitivity to comprehend and cope with life's challenges more adequately. How, precisely, does a liberal arts education convey these intangible benefits?

Alberta Arthurs's (1981, p. 43) essay provides one example. As her students analyzed the story of Lancelot and Guinevere, the story of the demise of King Arthur's Round Table and all that it stood for, "they . . . discovered that . . . echoes and anticipations of the final tragedy demonstrate the inevitability of that tragedy. . . . The students discovered . . . that passions, unrestrained and unchallenged, repeat and intensify and finally destroy. It is the passionate attachment of Guinevere and Lancelot, the passionate hatred of their enemies, even the passionate ambition of the good king, that are played out over and over in these paralleled scenes. Unexamined and unchecked, the passions accelerate into tragedy and into the death of a society. Private passions finally outweigh public purposes, and irrationality reigns in Arthur's kingdom."

Helen Vendler (1981, p. 350) speaks of similar aims in teaching literature: to save her students from a life "unaccompanied by a sense that others have also gone through it, and have left a record of their experience." She argues that a knowledge of Oedipus, Hamlet, Job, Antigone, and Jesus is essential "in order to refer private experience to some identifying frame or solacing reflection." Literature thus guides us through example, showing us in practical ways what it means to be a virtuous person in everyday relationships and situations.

Limits of the Purist Tradition

The arguments against practical training are received with understanding and joy by the defenders of that tradition in higher education that stresses knowledge for its own sake and that demands that education be devoted to human development rather than skills acquisition. Yet this tradition, too, has the defects in its virtues. It often has served as a self-serving ideology. Knowledge for its own sake has been a refuge of those seeking justification for the theory of the leisure class, even the superior power and privilege of that class (Bell, 1973; Bellah and others, 1985).

Moreover, this idea is very much akin in its implications to the "value-free, neutral scientist" approach fashionable among social scientists until quite recently. Such an idea amounts to an abrogation of responsibility for the interpretation and application of one's work (Friedrichs, 1970; Haan, Bellah, Rabinow, and Sullivan, 1983; MacRae, 1976; MacIntyre, 1984; Skiff, 1980). Carried to its logical extreme, the single-minded pursuit of knowledge for its own sake has resulted in the fragmentation of knowledge, a situation in which a general education and the solution of problems requiring a multidisciplinary approach (as most do) become impossible. Stephen Toulmin (1982, pp. 209–210) suggests that "we can no longer view the world as Descartes and Laplace would have us do, as 'rational onlookers,' from outside. Our place is within the same world that we are studying, and whatever scientific understanding we achieve must be a kind of understanding that is available to participants within the processes of nature, i.e., from the inside."

This abrogation extends to the realm of teaching as well, for even those advocates of knowledge for its own sake who bother with undergraduate teaching seldom deign discuss how that knowledge could be put to practical use. The advocates of pure knowledge share with the advocates of practical training an exceedingly narrow definition of *practical*. Yet, are not Alberta Arthurs's and Helen Vendler's attempts to enrich their students' lives through literature eminently practical? With respect to the discipline of sociology, Hans O. Mauksch argues: "Beyond the traditional role of teaching understanding and critique, exists the opportunity of using instruction as preparation for application and practice. It should be an emphatically held view that an occupational and application orientation in the teaching of sociology can, and indeed should, be undertaken within the framework of . . . the craft style of doing sociology. . . . Teaching future lawyers about law as a product of social structure and power can integrate scholarly concern with practical issues. Students planning to use a baccalaureate in sociology as community service workers or within the industrial or commercial world can learn concepts within the best traditions of sociology as a craft and yet have the organization of such teaching focused on practical application and on the translation of theoretical understanding to the demands of the world of work" (1980, p. 10).

Though the practical implication is the bete noire of purists, even more crass is any attempt to advise students on careers or jobs. Purists defend this view in two ways: (1) The pressure to choose a career early in the college years, imposed by our culture through the mediation of parents, is already excessive; it is "unfair to students as individuals, subversive to education values, and thoroughly unfortunate as social policy. If so, we probably ought to do more than we now do to shore up the frail and precarious confidence some students feel in their education, the pri-

Table 1. 1971-1981 Graduates of the College of Arts and Sciences, University of Virginia

Clarity of Career Goals at Graduation	Percentage Very Satisfied with First Job
Extremely unclear	10
Unclear	12
Somewhat unclear	17
Clear	20
Very clear	41

Source: Adapted from Kingston and Nock, 1985, p. 43.

mary thing for now, and the use to which they will put it as a secondary thing" (Jager, 1981, p. 89); and (2) even granting the legitimacy of students' and parents' career concerns, professors do not have the expertise to advise students in these ways. Besides, most colleges and universities have placement centers that have such expertise, and job hunting is a relatively simple matter, especially since placement centers provide opportunities for job interviews. Purists take at most a laissez-faire attitude toward their students' futures. What are the consequences of this attitude?

For one thing, it guarantees that students may have no clear idea of what they want or can do upon graduation. Consequently, they fumble from job to job until, if they are very lucky, they may discover meaningful work for themselves. Such stumbling early in one's career puts a person irretrievably behind one's peers (Ritzer and Walczak, 1986; Stumpf, 1984). Consider some results from the University of Virginia's survey of the 1971-1981 graduates of its College of Arts and Sciences (Kingston and Nock, 1985), as shown in Table 1. Graduates with clear career goals at graduation were more likely to report more job satisfaction with their first jobs. Moreover, this dramatic linkage between clarity of career direction and satisfaction does not entirely disappear later in life, for those with greater career direction at graduation were more satisfied with their present jobs as well. Finally, clarity of career goals was found to be positively linked with salary levels of both first and present jobs.

What about the purists' argument that they do not have the expertise to advise students, but that placement centers do? The first part of this argument has a certain superficial plausibility, but it is in fact incorrect. The most severe problems that liberal arts students face in hunting for jobs is that they are unable to specify for employers what they can do in terms of either widely transferable functional skills (reading, writing) or more specific discipline-based skills, such as foreign languages, computer programming, or organizational analysis. Only the discipline itself can provide employers with a list of the skills and abilities that its typical graduates acquire; it is folly to assume that either students or placement centers can do this. (Details on how faculty can develop such a skill listing can be found in Crittenden's, n.d., paper on developing a "collective resume.") Moreover, placement centers typically are not the major source of jobs for students (Granovetter, 1974; Lin, Ensel, and Vaughan, 1981; Kingston and Nock, 1985). Rather, most jobs are found through contacts: either personal acquaintances of students and their parents or contacts acquired through professors, summer jobs, internship and work-study programs more often arranged by a professor.

Our own research, which has sought to investigate the impact of a program of career advising and internships, has demonstrated a number of positive employment outcomes (Green, Klug, Neider, and Salem, 1981). A survey of those who graduated from our liberal arts program between the years 1970 and 1982 found that those who chose an internship placement as compared to those who did not (or for whom none was available if they had graduated before 1975) reported that they: (1) had less trouble finding jobs; (2) had greater job satisfaction; (3) saw their university education as having helped them become more effective in their work; and (4) had more prestigious and responsible jobs (Green and Salem, 1983).

Of parallel interest is the impact of responsible jobs on personal development. Kohn and Schooler (1978) have explored the reciprocal relationships between the nature of the job and the psychological functioning of the individual. A key concept in their work is the "substantive complexity" of the job, which they define as "the degree to which performance of the work requires thought and independent judgement" (p. 30). To understand the relationship between job complexity and personal social psychological qualities they have done extensive analysis of data from a panel surveyed in 1964 and again in 1974. To determine "substantive complexity" they measure the reported complexity of individuals' work with "things," "data," and "people," classifications much like those developed in the *Dictionary of Occupational Titles*. In the analysis of the data they use worker-supplied information on the jobs held prior to 1964, in 1964, and in 1974 to understand the possible changes in the individual psychological functioning of the respondent in conjunction with the changes in substantive complexity of the job. They find that substantive complexity is negatively correlated with "routinization" and "closeness of supervision" but positively correlated with "ideational flexibility." They conclude that individuals "who are self-directed in their work are consistently more likely to become non-authoritarian, to develop personally more responsible standards of morality, to become self-confident and not self-deprecatory, to become less fatalistic, less anxious and less conformist in their ideas" (Kohn and Schooler, 1978, p. 51). Thus the kinds of managerial and professional jobs for which we prepare our students actually support and reinforce the personal characteristics that we seek to instill through liberal education.

In addition, careful attention by faculty to advising and other out-of-classroom contacts with students can have a number of more immediate beneficial educational outcomes. For example, based on his critical review and synthesis of the research conducted on the relationship between informal, nonclassroom, student-faculty contact and college outcomes, Pascarella (1980) concluded that "with the influence of student preenrollment traits held constant, significant positive associations exist between the extent and quality of student-faculty informal contact and students' educational aspirations, their attitudes toward college, their academic achievement, intellectual and personal development, and their institutional persistence" (p. 590).

Finally, just as the emphasis on "knowledge for its own sake" can be perverted into a self-serving and socially irresponsible ideology, so too can the related demand that a "truly" liberal education must serve the needs of individual human development. To the extent that a liberal education is presumed to serve the developmental needs of individuals *only*, it thereby risks becoming a form of narcissistic therapy. In their perceptive book, *Habits of the Heart*, Robert Bellah and his colleagues (Bellah and others, 1985) offer a critique of the culture of therapy that is equally applicable to the aforementioned education-for-human-development view: "The belief that personal growth goes on endlessly and in any direction points up the ultimately aimless nature of the organic metaphor in such post-Freudian therapeutic hands. What is not questioned is the institutional context. One's 'growth' is a purely private matter. It may involve maneuvering within the structure of bureacratic rules and roles, changing jobs, maybe even changing spouses if necessary. But what is missing is any collective context in which one might act as a participant to change the institutional structures that frustrate and limit. Therapy's 'democratic side' lacks any public forum. Its freedom is closer to the free choice of market economy than to the shared argument and action of free citizens in a republic" (pp. 126–127).

Summary and Conclusions

Implicit in *Liberal Learning and Careers* (Green and Salem, 1981) was the argument that the two traditions that have fought for dominance in shaping American higher education, knowledge for its own sake versus practical training, ought to be viewed not as polar opposites but as opposites that are inextricably linked. When either tradition is emphasized at the expense of the other, it takes on defects in its virtues. Thus, resolving the conflict between these two traditions requires not a choice but rather a synthesis.

We are saddened to report that the recent critiques of American higher education still raise this old controversy. Their analyses overlook

16

the facts that ways of synthesizing the two traditions have already been proposed, are already successful, and are gaining wide use. Our 1981 volume, in the best spirit of the *New Directions* series, described or foreshadowed many of those ways.

For much of the 1980s the liberal arts have been undergoing a renaissance, seen in many realms inside and outside the academy. Medical schools are increasingly seeking applicants who are broadly educated, rather than those prepared in traditional premed curricula that focus on the life and natural sciences to the exclusion of the rest of the curriculum. The same is true of other graduate programs in the professions, notably nursing, law, business, engineering, and education. The accreditation associations of these professions are beginning to insist that their schools build in significant liberal arts components in their undergraduate curricula—either by hiring faculty prepared in liberal arts disciplines to offer courses "in house" or by drawing on the existing liberal arts curricula in their institutions (*Forum for Liberal Education*, 1982; Fowler, 1987a; Behrman and Levine, 1984). Curriculum reforms stressing interdisciplinary connections have become widespread (Heller, 1987). Enrollments in the liberal arts are up, as is the hiring of liberal arts faculty (Heller, 1986). Liberal learning in 1988 contends from a much stronger position than it did earlier in the decade. The survival of liberal arts departments and curricula seems less tied to "merger" with career-oriented programs. Yet, the theme of synthesizing the no less persistent traditions of liberal and practical learning continues to be the best prospect for the undergraduate curriculum.

References

Adelman, C. *The Standardized Test Scores of College Graduates, 1964-1982*. Washington, D.C.: Educational Resources Information Center, U.S. Department of Education, 1986.

Arthurs, A. "What Higher Education Has to Offer Business." In C. S. Green III and R. G. Salem (eds.), *Liberal Learning and Careers*. New Directions for Teaching and Learning, no. 6. San Francisco: Jossey-Bass, 1981.

Association of American Colleges. *Integrity in the College Curriculum*. Washington, D.C.: Association of American Colleges, 1985.

Beck, R. E. *Career Patterns: The Liberal Arts Major in Bell System Management*. Washington, D.C.: American Association of Colleges, 1981.

Behrman, J. H., and Levine, R. I. "Are Business Schools Doing Their Job?" *Harvard Business Review*, 1984, *84*, 140-147.

Bell, D. *The Coming of Post-Industrial Society*. New York: Basic Books, 1973.

Bellah, R. N., Madsen, R., Sullivan, W. M., Swidler, A., and Tipton, S. M. *Habits of the Heart*. New York: Harper & Row, 1985.

Bendix, R., and Berger, B. "Images of Society and Problems of Concept Formation in Sociology." In L. Gross (ed.), *Symposium on Sociological Theory*. New York: Harper & Row, 1959.

Bennett, W. J. *To Reclaim a Legacy*. Washington, D.C.: U.S. Government Printing Office, 1984.

Bloom, A. *The Closing of the American Mind.* New York: Simon & Schuster, 1987.

Bok, D. "Toward Education of Quality." *Harvard Magazine,* May-June 1986, pp. 49-64.

Boyer, E. L. *College: The Undergraduate Experience in America.* New York: Harper & Row, 1987.

Brann, E.T.H. *Paradoxes of Education in a Republic.* Chicago: University of Chicago Press, 1979.

Carnegie Foundation for the Advancement of Teaching. *College: The Undergraduate Experience in America.* New York: Harper & Row, 1987.

Crittenden, K. S. *What Our Graduates Have to Offer Employers: The Collective Resume.* Chicago: Department of Sociology, University of Illinois at Chicago, n.d.

Dictionary of Occupational Titles. (4th ed.) Washington, D.C.: U.S. Government Printing Office, 1977.

Forum for Liberal Education, 1982, *4* (6), entire issue.

Fowler, E. M. "Careers: More Need for Liberal Arts Seen." *New York Times,* Jan. 6, 1987a.

Fowler, E. M. "Careers: Industry's New Focus on 'Ethics.' " *New York Times,* Aug. 11, 1987b.

Friedrichs, R. W. *A Sociology of Sociology.* New York: Free Press, 1970.

Granovetter, M. S. *Getting a Job.* Cambridge, Mass.: Harvard University Press, 1974.

Green, C. S., III, Klug, H. G., Neider, L. A., and Salem, R. G. "Careers, Curricula, and the Future of Liberal Learning: A Program for Action." In C. S. Green III and R. G. Salem (eds.), *Liberal Learning and Careers.* New Directions for Teaching and Learning, no. 6. San Francisco: Jossey-Bass, 1981.

Green, C. S., III, and Salem, R. G. (eds.). *Liberal Learning and Careers.* New Directions for Teaching and Learning, no. 6. San Francisco: Jossey-Bass, 1981.

Green, C. S., III, and Salem, R. G. "The Nonsociologist as Applied Sociologist: Teaching Undergraduate Applied Sociology as Ethical Practice." *Teaching Sociology,* 1983, *11* (1), 32-46.

Guest, R. H. "Industrial Sociology: The Competitive Edge." *Footnotes* (Newsletter of the American Sociological Association), Jan. 1987, p. 5-7.

Haan, N., Bellah, R. N., Rabinow, P., and Sullivan, W. M. (eds.). *Social Science as Moral Inquiry.* New York: Columbia University Press, 1983.

Heller, S. "Job Market for Professors in English and Foreign Languages Shows Vigor." *Chronicle of Higher Education,* Dec. 10, 1986, p. 1.

Heller, S. "A New Wave of Curricular Reform." *Chronicle of Higher Education,* Sept. 2, 1987, p. A28-34.

Hirsch, E. D. *Cultural Literacy.* Boston: Houghton Mifflin, 1987.

Jacoby, J. E., Pugh, M. D., Snyder, E. E., and Spreitzer, E. A. "There Is Life (and Work) After Sociology." *Teaching Sociology,* 1984, *11* (4), 399-417.

Jager, R. "Career and Curriculum: A Philosophical Critique." In C. S. Green III and R. G. Salem (eds.), *Liberal Learning and Careers.* New Directions for Teaching and Learning, no. 6. San Francisco: Jossey-Bass, 1981.

Jefferson, T. *Writings.* New York: Literary Classics of the United States, 1984.

Kingston, P. W., and Nock, S. L. "The Careers of Recent College Graduates." Unpublished manuscript, Department of Sociology, University of Virginia, 1985.

Kohn, M. L., and Schooler, C. "The Reciprocal Effects of the Substantive Complexity of Work and Intellectual Flexibility: A Longitudinal Assessment." *American Journal of Sociology,* 1978, *84,* 24-52.

Kohn, M. L., and Schooler, C. *Work and Personality.* New York: Ablex Press, 1983.

Lin, W., Ensel, W. M., and Vaughan, J. C. "Social Resources and the Strength of Ties: Structural Factors in Occupational Status Attainment." *American Sociological Review*, 1981, *46*, 393-405.

Litt, E. "Higher Education and the American Political Economy." In C. S. Green III and R. G. Salem (eds.), *Liberal Learning and Careers.* New Directions for Teaching and Learning, no. 6. San Francisco: Jossey-Bass, 1981.

MacIntyre, A. *After Virtue.* (2nd ed.) Notre Dame, Ind.: University of Notre Dame Press, 1984.

MacRae, D., Jr. *The Social Function of Social Science.* New Haven, Conn.: Yale University Press, 1976.

Mauksch, H. O. "Sociological Craftmanship and the Opportunities of Sociology." *Wisconsin Sociologist*, 1980, *17* (1), 9-11.

Mauksch, H. O., and Howery, C. B. "Social Change for Teaching: The Case of One Disciplinary Association." *Teaching Sociology*, 1986, *14*, 73-82.

Maxfield, B. D., and Belisle, M. *Science, Engineering, and Humanities Doctorates in the United States: 1983 Profile.* Washington, D.C.: National Academy Press, 1985.

National Institute of Education. *Involvement in Learning: Realizing the Potential of American Higher Education.* Washington, D.C.: U.S. Government Printing Office, 1984.

Otten, A. L. "Ethics on the Job." *Wall Street Journal*, July 14, 1986, p. 1.

Pascarella, E. T. "Student-Faculty Informal Contact and College Outcomes." *Review of Educational Research*, 1980, *50* (4), 545-595.

Ritzer, G., and Walczak, D. *Working: Conflict and Change.* (3rd ed.) Englewood Cliffs, N.J.: Prentice-Hall, 1986.

Rohatyn, F. "Ethics in America's Money Culture." *New York Times*, June 3, 1987, p. A27.

Rossi, P. H. "The Presidential Address: The Challenge and Opportunities of Applied Social Research." *American Sociological Review*, 1980, *45*, 889-904.

Shad, J.S.R. "Business's Bottom Line: Ethics." *New York Times*, July 27, 1987, p. A19.

Skiff, A. "Toward a Theory of Publishing or Perishing." *American Sociologist*, 1980, *15*, 175-183.

Solmon, L. C. "Exploring the Link Between College Education and Work." In C. S. Green III and R. G. Salem (eds.), *Liberal Learning and Careers.* New Directions for Teaching and Learning, no. 6. San Francisco: Jossey-Bass, 1981.

Stricharchuk, G. "Businesses Crack Down on Workers Who Cheat to Help the Company." *Wall Street Journal*, June 13, 1986, p. 1.

Stumpf, S. A. "Adult Career Development: Individual and Organizational Factors." In N. C. Gysbers and Associates, *Designing Careers: Counseling to Enhance Education, Work, and Leisure.* San Francisco: Jossey-Bass, 1984.

Toulmin, S. *The Return to Cosmology: Postmodern Science and the Theology of Nature.* Berkeley: University of California Press, 1982.

Toward the Restoration of the Liberal Arts Curriculum. New York: Rockefeller Foundation, 1979.

Vendler, H. "Presidential Address 1980." *Proceedings of the Modern Language Association*, 1981, *96*, 350.

Whyte, W. F. "Social Inventions for Solving Human Problems." *American Sociological Review*, 1982, *47*, 1-13.

Charles S. Green III and Richard G. Salem are both professors of sociology at the University of Wisconsin–Whitewater.

While teachers in American colleges and universities, as a result of forces in both society and their profession, find it difficult to raise the question of moral judgment with students, the methods and implications of their disciplines suggest a way of doing so.

Moral Judgment and College Curricula

Michael J. Collins

During the week of July 5, 1987, as Lieutenant Colonel Oliver North gave testimony before the congressional committees investigating the Iran-contra affair, some three miles across the city Georgetown University was hosting its annual Alumni College, a week-long program of short courses, lectures, and trips in and around Washington for alumni and parents. But Oliver North was not the only show in town that week. Daniel Berrigan, S.J., the best known member of the Catonsville nine and most recently an actor, with Jeremy Irons and Robert De Niro, in Roland Joffe's *The Mission*, came to Georgetown (the evening before he was arrested, with Martin Sheen, at the Riverside Research Institute in New York) to talk about the film in both its historic and contemporary contexts. At the same time, just a few blocks south of the Capitol, the Acting Company at Arena Stage was in its final week of Zelda Fichandler's superb production of Arthur Miller's *The Crucible*. As many alumni and parents commented, Georgetown University, set on a hilltop over the city of Washington, was an intriguing place to be taking classes that week.

Moral Judgment in America

Among the events of Alumni College was a trip to see *The Crucible* (Miller, 1976) a play that speaks with great insight of the American exper-

R. E. Young, K. E. Eble (eds.). *College Teaching and Learning: Preparing for New Commitments.*
New Directions for Teaching and Learning, no. 33. San Francisco: Jossey-Bass, Spring 1988.

iment in democracy. The central figure of the play, a farmer named John Proctor, in a scene whose staging coincidentally recalled the interrogations at the Capitol that afternoon, appears before the General Court of Salem to prove his friends innocent of witchcraft and ends up condemned to death himself. Like so many American heroes before him—Frederick Henry, who makes a separate peace by leaping into the Tagliamento River; the marshal in *High Noon*, who must, despite the pleading of his bride, fight alone the desperadoes who threaten his town; Huckleberry Finn, who discovers he "can't pray a lie" and so goes off to steal his friend Jim out of slavery—John Proctor finds himself set radically apart from the community of which he has been a member. In the end, he faces an austere and difficult choice: He can either pray a lie, confess to witchcraft, and live; or he can speak the truth, continue to profess his innocence, and die.

In the last act, moments before he is to be hanged, because it seems politically expedient that he do so, the deputy governor gives Proctor one last chance to confess. His wife, Elizabeth, is brought from prison, and the Reverend Mr. Hale, who has come to recognize the obscene injustice of the witch trials, pleads with her to convince him to lie (Miller, 1976, p. 132): "Quail not before God's judgment in this, for it may well be God Damns a liar less than he that throws his life away for pride. . . . Woman, before the laws of God we are as swine! We cannot read His will!" But Elizabeth makes no judgment, and as her husband tries desperately to know whether the right choice is life or death, she identifies him as a characteristically American figure, the man alone who must as Natty Bumppo might say, follow his own gifts, the American Protestant who can look only to his own conscience for guidance (p. 137): "There be no higher judge under Heaven than Proctor is!" Elizabeth here voices the terrifying and dangerous Emersonian doctrine, the one that animates all American heroes and defines their heroism (p. 147): "To believe your own thought, to believe that what is true for you in your private heart is true for all men—that is genius."

Proctor decides initially to confess, but in the end, he cannot sign his statement and is led away to be hanged. While the final impact of the play in production, the energy it generates on the stage, makes its closing moments a celebration of John Proctor's heroism and ultimately overrides Mr. Hale's earlier critique of Emersonian self-reliance, his words, "we cannot read His will" (p. 132), ought not, outside the theater, be dismissed. John Proctor goes to his death convinced, like so many American heroes before him, that his truth, no matter what society at large might say, is God's truth, a conviction that American authors have always seemed particularly ready to affirm.

Whether consciously or instinctively, Colonel North seemed aware that week, as did Daniel Berrigan when he wrote *The Trial of the Catons-*

ville Nine, just what American heroes are made of, just how Americans are accustomed to define heroes. While he insisted to the congressional investigators that "I was authorized to do everything that I did," he also portrayed himself as a patriot alone with his conscience, a man who had to do what he had to do to keep the world safe for democracy. "I did a lot of things and I want to stand up and say that I'm proud of them. . . . Lying does not come easy to me. But we all had to weigh in the balance the difference between lives and lies" (Magnuson, 1987, p. 18). The investigation on Capitol Hill was as dramatic an event as *The Crucible* down the street at Arena Stage. Colonel North drew more viewers that week than the soap operas usually do; "Thank you, Oliver North" bumper stickers appeared around the country; letters and telegrams to the offices of the congressional investigators ran twenty to one in his favor (Magnuson, 1987). As Daniel Berrigan, who had been imprisoned for destroying draft records in 1968, spoke at Georgetown about the history of oppression in Latin America, Oliver North, a wounded veteran of the war in Vietnam, testified before a congressional committee to his efforts to end oppression in Nicaragua. The coincidence of Colonel North and Father Berrigan together in Washington during a run of *The Crucible* pointed to a larger question, one that has troubled America throughout its history and (if we remember Socrates in *Crito*, for example) one that would trouble any democracy: How can you know whose sticker to put on your bumper? Emerson's answer in "Self-Reliance" is not very comforting. When reminded that the "impulses" of the self-reliant individual "may be from below, not from above" he says, with fine American innocence, "they do not seem to me to be such, but if I am the Devil's child, I will live then from the Devil" (Whicher, 1957, pp. 149–150).

The Problem in Colleges and Universities

If the stories of Colonel North and Father Berrigan (as well as John Proctor and Mr. Hale) recall the difficulty of giving answers to significant moral questions, they also suggest the obstacles colleges and universities face in bringing students to grapple with such questions in all their inevitable complexity and ambiguity. The faculty at most colleges and universities in America these days is little more than a collection of individuals whose allegiance is not to a particular institution with a distinct vision, mission, or goal, but to a discipline, to the profession, to research and publication. (The ease with which successful scholars settle into new positions suggests that they feel little commitment to particular institutions and that the institutions themselves, no matter what claims their undergraduate catalogues may make, rarely have a distinct vision of education or a corporate way of implementing it.) And paradoxically, a college or university is more likely to reward with tenure and promotion those who serve the discipline rather than those who serve the institution and the students it has committed itself to teach. Scholars are, of necessity, by the nature of their lonely, specialized, intensely private projects, individuals who work alone or, in the case of some scientists, in small and isolated groups. The specialized work, its narrow focus, the reluctance of most scholars to generalize very widely from particulars or to write for anyone but other scholars all conspire to make corporate efforts unlikely, to turn a faculty into a collection of individuals who do not share the same interests or even speak the same language. The situation probably will not change: The young men and women who are now beginning to teach in colleges and universities seem even more committed to the narrow, value-free scholarship that is published (if not entirely honored) in most disciplines these days. And who can blame them? They have been taught that such work alone is scholarly and worthwhile, and even if they are not convinced, a commitment to it is their only way to survive in a world they never made.

But teachers—and, for that matter, administrators—whether they like it or not, teach by example. While some give generous time and loving attention to their students, too many do not, often because, even when they want to, they realize that it simply does not pay to do so, that it is essentially suicidal. As a result, students are not only poorly served by their college or university, but they are also implicitly taught that it is wiser to take care of yourself than to take care of others, to keep your own career firmly on track, to accrue salary (such as it is in education), prestige, and above all the security of tenure, despite the compromises you may have to make, despite the indifference or neglect with which you may have to treat the young men and women who have been entrusted to you. The lesson is driven home clearly and dramatically each time a college or university denies a generous and effective teacher tenure and offers it instead to one who has chosen to emphasize publication over teaching.

The arguments are familiar. Scholarship and teaching are complementary, not inimical (although studies of personality suggest that one person would rarely feel the same enthusiasm for both). The prestige of the institution and the quality of its intellectual life are enhanced by the work of its scholars. Teaching and scholarship are weighed equally in decisions on promotion and tenure. Too often a generous and effective teacher is denied tenure because his or her publications have not reached some quantitative standard. Too often publication is what truly matters, and any teaching is judged adequate for those who (like pieceworkers in a factory) produce. Some students, at least, learn well the lessons their colleges and universities teach them. These days they are glad to see the scholars tenured because the prestige of the institution (they believe) will be enhanced and their degrees, as a result, will be worth more in the marketplace. Although the reputation of most institutions in the world at large has finally little to do with the publications of its faculty (which are typically esoteric, narrowly focused, and addressed to other specialists), the faculty, the administration, and the students together denigrate the value of teaching and reward those who care primarily for their own scholarly careers. How can anyone in a college or university be outraged, disappointed, or even surprised that too many young men and women in America these days pursue their own careers with single-minded (and often self-destructive) determination and, unaware of any communal claims upon them, focus, to the exclusion of all else, on satisfying their own needs and desires?

For a variety of reasons then, those who teach in colleges and universities are reluctant to raise with their students, through the material of their courses, serious moral questions. Scholarship, at least as it is generally practiced in America, does not concern itself with such questions because, so the argument goes, they are not scholarly questions. To raise them in a classroom would be to leave the ground one has struggled to tame and enter a wilderness. At the same time, the scholar, whose voice in the institution is simply one among the variegated many, shares with his fellow Americans a reluctance not so much to propose answers to moral questions, as to argue, as he or she might have to in the classroom, that some answers are better than others. With neither community nor scholarship to support them, most teachers, it seems, would prefer not to raise moral questions, for by doing so they might ultimately have to say (unscientifically, impolitely, undemocratically—with both humility and conviction): Having "wept and fasted, wept and prayed," having struggled through the complexities and ambiguities of this human situation in an existential world, I believe my answer to be good and true. In colleges and universities, as too often in society at large, the Emersonian dilemma of above and below gets solved by leveling everything to "I'm O.K., you're O.K." But as recent events in Washington, Wall Street, and Denver should make clear, that's not O.K. The abiding human questions must be answered, even as we know the answers are always provisional, subject to revision, spoken in words that are halting, tentative, guarded, even as we recognize, with Kant (1934, p. 38), that "human reason . . . is burdened by questions which . . . by the very nature of reason itself, it is not able to ignore, but which . . . it is also not able to answer." While the relativism of "I'm O.K., you're O.K." seems debilitating and, in a world where choices will inevitably be made, finally naive and unrealistic, dogma and absolutism, as Kant suggests, is not the answer either. What is needed is a way of freeing teachers and students from either the presumption of absolutism or the inertia of relativism.

Making Moral Judgments

While I shall come back to Kant's questions later, I should like for a moment to propose that teaching can itself provide an example of the way in which all men and women struggle toward the moral judgments they must inevitably make as they seek to live wisely and justly in a complex, ambiguous world. In 1981, I saw two excellent productions of Athol Fugard's great play, *A Lesson from Aloes*—one at the Playhouse Theater in New York, the other at Arena Stage in Washington. Set, as all of Fugard's plays, in South Africa, it tells the story of a white couple, Piet and Gladys Bezuidenhout, and Steve Daniels, their colored friend. In each production the script was the same. As the play draws to its close, Steve leaves reluctantly for England in order to escape his banning order and, as he puts it, to "feed and clothe my family" (p. 70). Gladys packs her suitcase to return to the mental institution where she was hospitalized after the secret police had read and confiscated her diaries. In the end, as Fugard writes in the stage direction, "Piet, in the backyard, sits with the unidentified aloe" (p. 83), one whose name he had tried to determine at the beginning of the play.

While it would have been entirely possible to end the play with Piet sitting motionless in the backyard, neither director (Fugard in New York and Douglas C. Wager in Washington) did so. In Washington, Stanley Anderson dropped to his knees and, still holding the aloe, wept so violently that his body shook. In New York, Harris Yulin raised his head from the aloe and looked up, out over the audience. With Stanley Anderson, the play ended in despair, looking back upon itself and saying that hope is impossible. With Harris Yulin, it ended not with joy certainly, but, for all the cruelty and suffering it had portrayed, with a guarded act of faith in the enduring goodness and dignity of human life, in the quiet joy that love can sometimes bring to men and women, in possibility for the future.

When I describe the two endings to students, they inevitably want to know which one is right. While some would say a teacher should never answer such a question, I always do, for I believe that if the play is worth the time we spend on it in the classroom, then the answer is important and not just a matter of opinion or desire. The right answer, I tell them, is the one that articulates better the play's judgment on the world it portrays, the one that seems to say in its final moment, in its final gesture or movement, what all the preceding moments of the play have said together. The answer to the question lies in the script, and it can be gotten only by reading it with as much care and sensitivity as possible, by facing its complex and inevitably ambiguous design with honesty, tenacity, and courage, by letting it speak its understanding of the human condition as it will, no matter what the reader (or the director) may believe or desire. When students ask me which ending to *A Lesson from Aloes* is right, I tell them the one Harris Yulin gave it in New York, not because it reflects more nearly than Stanley Anderson's what I believe and desire to be true about the world, but because after reading the script as honestly and carefully as I can, it seems to me to have said what the play in its sequence of moments says, to have made the act of faith that the particulars of the play themselves make. We can have no certitudes, in the script or in the world its reflects, the one we all return to when we leave the theater or the classroom. All we can do anywhere is read with care and make what seem the right choices along the way. Whatever we can finally say, whatever answers we can finally make must always be earned—in the classroom and theater through a complex and recalcitrant script, in the world through the ambiguities and complications of an existential dispensation.

As I have tried to suggest, one way to teach students to make difficult moral judgments, one way to help them toward some answers to the truly important human questions is to teach them to interpret, carefully and honestly, whatever texts or data the discipline deals with, to come to considered judgments upon them. The processes are analogous. In the case of *A Lesson from Aloes,* one ending is better than the other if one ending speaks better the meaning of its particulars, the cumulative impact of its sequential moments on the audience. The process by which we come to judgment on the play is the complex and difficult process of reading the script, of submitting ourselves to its demands while knowing that, to the extent it remains true to the existential complication of the world it reflects, it will resist and finally defeat our best efforts to interpret it, to articulate, in all its rich complexity, the meaning of its particulars.

We come to the script with the expectation that it will make sense, that its particulars will cohere in an intelligible pattern, that we may finally read and speak its vision. In the interplay of that comforting expectation and the complex, ambiguous, recalcitrant script, we find whatever meaning we can. The answers we make are necessarily tentative and provisional (Douglas C. Wager saw in *A Lesson from Aloes* something that I do not), but at the same time they have been earned, shaped, and formulated by an honest, tenacious, even courageous submission to the script, the text, or, in other disciplines, to the data, to the discoveries of the laboratory or the library. In the same way, any answer we make to such difficult human questions as what should a man or a woman die for, lie for, go to prison for has to be earned in the existential complication of a complex, ambiguous world, in the interplay of what we believe to be good with the often conflicting demands of a particular human situation so that, once again, we may say, with both humility and conviction, I believe this answer to be good and true. The process by which we come to judgment in the disciplines we teach is analogous to the process by which men and women come to judgment in the world those disciplines reflect and seek to understand. The teacher who struggles to answer such a question as how to end *A Lesson from Aloes* (rather than simply listing the various answers the critics provide) offers his or her students, by example, a way of moving toward judgment in the serious human situations they will inevitably face outside the classroom.

Raising the Important Questions

The words "what we believe to be good" (which recall Emerson as well as Daniel Berrigan and Oliver North, John Proctor, and Mr. Hale), make clear that something more than a process is needed. If we who teach are to help our students to make wise moral judgments, then we must bring them, through our teaching, through the insights of our disciplines, to confront and find some answers to the old Socratic question: How is one to live wisely and justly in a society of men and women on a fragile planet the one life he or she is given to live? The question is inherent in the work of every discipline, and it will, if we allow it, emerge naturally in any classroom. It is a disturbing question, no doubt, both in the classroom and in the world outside, for it transcends all our powers to answer it. And yet we all of us do answer it, consciously or unconsciously, in the particular choices we make every day of our lives. In a play like *A Lesson from Aloes* (Fugard, 1981), as we hear Gladys, after describing her horrifying shock treatments at the mental hospital, say to Steven, "they've burned my brain as brown as yours" (p. 80), we come to recognize, through the power of the play, not just that the question has meaning, but that some answers are better than others. We make trivial the disciplines we teach if we treat them like games of chess, engaging but ultimately irrelevant intellectual exercises, if we do not allow them to illuminate the struggle to discover how we are to live.

And beyond this question is still another, more difficult to raise, impossible, by its very nature, to answer, for it brings us to the edge of "the undiscovered country, from whose bourn/No traveler returns" (*Hamlet*, act 3, sc. 1, lines 79-80). Do we live finally in a sane or a lunatic universe? The question can never be answered, yet it must remain a question lest we and our students give way to the arrogant presumption of certitude or the debilitating despair of skepticism. "Do not despair: one of the thieves was saved. Do not presume: one of the thieves was damned" (Esslin, 1980, p. 53). As Samuel Beckett, quoting Saint Augustine, suggests here, all we can do is to live, poised between everything and nothing, the one life we have been given to live, a life that takes the question seriously and struggles to live out the implications of doing so. At the end of *A Lesson from Aloes*, as Harris Yulin looked out over the audience, the play gave one answer. Later that year, as Stanley Anderson dropped weeping to the stage, it gave another. Like many great works of literature, *A Lesson from Aloes* brings us to face that fundamental question: Do we live finally in a sane or a lunatic universe? If it gives no certain answer—either in the hands of a skillful director or for the world it reflects—it is because it remains, as any great work of literature must, true to the complexities and ambiguities of the existential world and so rests finally, as we all do, poised between everything and nothing, between presumption and despair. While we know their answers cannot in the end be discovered, we who teach must nonetheless ask our students (as we must ourselves) to take such questions as these two seriously so that when they are faced, as they inevitably are, with the necessity of making a choice, of deciding what is worth dying for, lying for, going to prison for, they will have some examined vision of what they believe to be good, some earned grounds upon which to make, with both humility and conviction, as wise a judgment as they can.

Such work for teachers is never easy. It puts them in uncharted territory to struggle continually with the existential complications, the ambiguities and complexities, of a fallen, fragile world. At the same time, the work must ordinarily be done alone, for the institution, the accepted terms of the discipline, and society at large all suggest it cannot (or even should not) be done. And yet what better way do we have than our disciplines, than the conversation of teacher, student, and material, to propose some answers to questions that must inevitably be answered?

References

Esslin, M. *The Theatre of the Absurd.* (3rd ed.) Harmondsworth, England: Penguin, 1980.

Fugard, A. *A Lesson from Aloes.* New York: Random House, 1981.

Kant, E. *Critique of Pure Reason.* (J.M.D. Meiklejohn, trans.) New York: Dutton, 1934.

Magnuson, E. "The 'Fall Guy' Fights Back." *Time,* July 20, 1987, pp. 16–25.

Miller, A. *The Crucible.* Harmondsworth, England: Penguin, 1976.

Ormond, J. *Selected Poems.* Bridgend, Wales: Poetry Wales Press, 1987.

Whicher, S. E. (ed.). *Selections from Ralph Waldo Emerson.* Boston: Houghton Mifflin, 1957.

Michael J. Collins is a member of the department of English and dean of the School for Summer and Continuing Education at Georgetown University.

Despite rapid developments in educational technology, teaching methods in postsecondary education remain remarkably traditional. However, the microcomputer has emerged as a powerful tool that is transforming what and how students learn, both inside and outside the classroom.

Technology and College Teaching

Christopher K. Knapper

Expanding Learning Through New Communications Technologies appeared under my editorship six years ago (Knapper, 1982), and my task here is to examine some of the technological developments that have affected teaching and learning in higher education since that volume was published in 1982.

Perhaps surprisingly, this is the only one of the past thirty issues in the New Directions for Teaching and Learning series that has had educational technology as a central theme. And, in fact, a quick check of the indexes of other volumes in the series reveals remarkably few references to the main technological innovations discussed in *Expanding Learning Through New Communications Technologies.* This might indicate a disdain for technology by those concerned with the improvement of teaching and learning in colleges and universities. Or, more plausibly, it might show that the major instructional issues and problems in higher education have more to do with underlying pedagogical principles than with hardware—a point I made in my concluding chapter of the 1982 volume.

Nonetheless, education has traditionally made quite extensive use of the products and processes of technology, from the chalkboard to the computer, and a vast amount continues to be written on the subject of

R. E. Young, K. E. Eble (eds.). *College Teaching and Learning: Preparing for New Commitments.*
New Directions for Teaching and Learning, no. 33. San Francisco: Jossey-Bass, Spring 1988.

instructional technology (the application of technology to teaching and learning). Indeed, some enthusiasts continue to look to a "technological fix" that might radically transform educational practice, making it both more effective and efficient.

Expanding Learning Through New Communications Technologies described a number of technologies that had been used in university teaching, or that appeared to have potential for the near future in higher education settings, including such innovations as cable television, the electronic blackboard, satellites, slow-scan TV, videodiscs, videotex and teletext, and of course a wide range of applications of computers, especially microcomputers. But not all chapters focused on a specific innovation. Rather, most contributors discussed educational approaches or themes, and posed questions about how developments in technology might lead to changes and improvements. One such theme was distance education, another simulation and gaming. A third involved access by students in the social sciences to complex data bases, while a fourth author discussed the relationship between technology and the promotion of lifelong learning.

In undertaking this retrospective review and update it is of course impossible to cover all those technological developments that could be of some relevance to higher education. Instead I will explore some issues in educational technology that seem to be of particular significance for the improvement of teaching and learning methods. My aim is to try to make links between what was regarded as important six years ago when *Expanding Learning Through New Technologies* was written, the perceived state of the art in 1988, and those developments that seem most desirable (or most likely) over the next six years.

Technological Aids for Teachers and Students

Classroom teaching has always made use of technological aids— sometimes developed especially for educational settings (such as the blackboard and overhead projector), but more commonly adapting technologies that were originally devised for other purposes. The most famous example of a successfully adapted technology is undoubtedly the movable-type printing press, which brought about a shift from a total reliance on the oral tradition in teaching to methods of learning and scholarship that depend primarily on the written word. Indeed Perkins (1985) has argued that the invention of printing produced fundamental changes in the way humans conceptualize the world and process information about it, with human memory becoming devalued in the face of widespread availability of printed records. He believes that the computer will bring about a similar cognitive transformation in the way we process information. A more recent innovation developed outside educational settings is the dry copier (Xerox machine), which again has had a surprisingly widespread (and often unrecognized) influence on the way educational information is disseminated.

Technology as a Primary Medium of Instruction

Most of the above examples, with the partial exception of print, refer to technologies used as supplements or aids to the principal communication medium, which is usually a human teacher. Of much more interest to educational technologies are approaches that can be used as an alternative to or substitute for traditional teaching—what might be called self-sufficient instructional technologies. An early example here is educational radio, used in some countries (for example, Australia) to serve remote students out of reach of a school.

Television. Later it was foreseen that television might play a comparable role, although this medium lacks radio's capacity for fairly simple two-way communication. Television has been used in the school and college system in two main ways: to relay what takes place in a regular live classroom to distant sites (either on or off campus) or in the form of self-contained programs that can be transmitted to school or homes and can be recorded on videotape for playback at the convenience of the learner. Somewhat surprisingly in view of its immense impact on popular culture, attitudes, and values, television has had a rather limited influence upon regular classroom settings. While this may be partly due to difficulties of projecting a large enough high-quality video image for easy viewing by more than a handful of students, there are also more fundamental reasons relating to the culture of the school and college classroom, in which the preferred prime initiator of information and instruction is a human teacher. On the other hand, television has played a much more prominent role in distance education, as described later in this chapter. In addition, a number of television-derived technologies have been incorporated into other instructional innovations, such as videotex and interactive-videodisc computer-aided instruction (CAI), also discussed below.

CAI and Its Variants. Because television was the dominant technology of the 1950s, it was natural that educators would see this medium as a powerful way of delivering instruction. Similarly, in the 1960s great efforts were made to develop instructional systems mediated by computers. Computer-assisted instruction (CAI) was first implemented on large mainframe machines almost twenty-five years ago, and the basic principles had been devised even earlier for teaching machines and programmed instruction. Although the teaching machine was looked to as a technology that would transform the school system (and replace many teachers), its main lasting impact was as a testbed for principles of instructional design that are still used in much contemporary CAI—such things as the specification of precise behavioral objectives, dividing instructional materials into manageable units, repeated testing of students' responses so as to devise appropriate remedial sequences and constantly fine-tune the program, and so on. Although from a pedagogical standpoint it could be argued that a good deal of currently available computer course-ware is inferior to early programmed instruction, the presentation capa-bilities of the modern microcomputer are far superior to those possible on a mechanical teaching machine.

There are many advantages claimed for CAI. It is an active form of learning that can be highly engaging and motivating. It is highly structured, tailored to individual learners' needs, "reversible" (learners can easily go back to the starting point), nonthreatening, and self-paced. It encourages self-management of learning and self-evaluation, allows repeated practice without instructor fatigue (is "tireless"), and provides constant feedback to learners on their success. It can keep detailed records of student progress and can expose the learner to situations and experi-ences that are not normally possible in a traditional classroom. Whether or not these benefits are realized depends, of course, on the instructional approach adopted. Some critics have cited disadvantages to computer-controlled learning—for example, that it may be too individualized and fail to take into account the important social context of the conventional college classroom.

Interestingly enough, no chapter in *Expanding Learning Through New Communications Technologies* was devoted exclusively to CAI, but the theme of instructional uses of computers—especially micro-computers—ran through most of the contributions to that volume. The earliest types of computer-based instruction involved drill and practice or tutorial programs, both of which employ the simple strategy of pres-enting information, posing a question that tests student mastery or com-prehension, and then proceeding to offer further instruction depending on the response. Such approaches still dominate today, especially in commercially available courseware.

Computer Simulations. A quite different strategy has been to use the computer as a way of simulating a particular situation, environment, or problem. This is the approach used in the very popular computer games and, at the other extreme, in such training devices as (computer-controlled) flight simulators. Computer simulations were discussed in the earlier volume by Mitchell. They have particular appeal in higher education settings, where it is often desirable to replicate in the classroom situations that would be impossible or difficult for students to experience firsthand. The popularity of educational simulations has increased as microcomputers have become more sophisticated, and it is now possible to incorporate moving graphics and sound, and to interact with the machine by means of joysticks, touch-screens, and so on, as well as via the keyboard. Medical simulations (for instance, where students can attempt diagnosis and treatment without danger to the patient) have been popular for many years, and there is a wide range of commercial packages available, especially simulations of laboratory assignments. Reasons for the popularity of the simulated lab may include the budgetary constraints facing many universities, with consequent lack of physical and human resources to run laboratories. It should also be noted that such packages do not generally serve as substitutes for the course instructor, who is still left firmly in control of the teaching situation. One concern that has been expressed about the wholesale substitution of simulated experiences for the "real" situation is that students may find it difficult to deal with the idiosyncrasies and unpredictable nature of comparable events in the external world, though this is clearly a matter of the ingenuity with which the simulation is devised.

Interactive Video. Interactive video refers to the marrying of the computer as an instructional control device with the use of a commercial videodisc player to present filmed or taped visual material that can comprise moving or still sequences. "Interactive" refers to the possibility for the learner to influence what is presented, depending on responses to questions posed by the instructional program. The potential of such an approach is considerable, especially where there is a need to demonstrate a process—for example, in industrial training settings. These and other experimental applications (many in the teaching of foreign language) were described by Nugent in *Expanding Learning Through New Communications Technologies.* Although the medium continues to attract interest among those working in CAI, there are still few successful commercial applications. Possible reasons include the difficulty and expense of making the master disc and the fact that videodisc players have never been the popular commercial success that many predicted. Hence as recently as two years ago one educator who had spent several years involved with this type of CAI still talked of its "remarkable potential" but expressed his disappointment with the quality of most videodisc-based instructional programs. "Although present knowledge about instructional design provides the basis for significant improvement in the quality of educational materials, there is a dearth of well-proven principles and procedures for the design of interactive videodisc systems for instructional purposes" (Taylor, 1985, p. 60). Once again, it appears that sound pedagogical applications of CAI lag behind technological accomplishments.

Artificial Intelligence and CAI. The application of artificial intelligence (AI) to computer-based instruction has been something of a Holy Grail sought by educational technologists for at least twenty years since Pask developed an "adaptive" teaching machine for use by Hollerith key-punch operators in the late 1950s (see Lewis, 1963). More recently,

Jones (1985) has reviewed educational applications of artificial intelligence or "intelligent computer-assisted instruction" (ICAI). Jones summarizes some of the perceived weaknesses in traditional CAI that artificial intelligence approaches might overcome. These include the inability of CAI to use the natural language of the student or to accept unanticipated responses (and hence to decide what is best taught next), lack of capacity to learn from the student's mistakes and misconceptions (and thus an inability to modify instructional strategies or learn new ones). In contrast, with ICAI the learner's interests and misunderstandings "drive the tutorial dialogue," using different teaching approaches for different students and employing natural "conversational" language (Jones, 1985, p. 518). ICAI can be seen as a type of coaching or true tutorial.

Clearly, to achieve this ideal in practice is a tall order. In the case of a live tutorial, the teaching strategies are generally subtle and implicit. Studying what happens in such situations (essentially an "expert systems" approach) is a complex, time-consuming business and has formed the basis for much of the work on ICAI. For example, SOPHIE (SOPHisticated Instructional Environment) is an ICAI system that teaches problem-solving skills in electronics. Learners try to identify faults in a piece of electrical equipment by taking various measurements and formulating hypotheses, with the program giving "coaching." According to Wheeler (1987), the first commercially available "intelligent tutor" (developed by researchers at Carnegie-Mellon University to teach the sophisticated programming language Lisp) went on the market in 1986.

In fact, there is a thin line between systems like SOPHIE that purport to be adaptive or "intelligent" and many simulations that also allow the students to seek information and try out solutions. The ability of the computer to "learn about" the student and modify its teaching strategy accordingly is simply a matter of degree. Ideally the instructional program would itself be modified on the basis of its teaching "experience" (a commonplace for most human teachers), but in practice this has rarely been attempted, except in experimental applications. Jones concludes that the systems she discusses "still fall short of what we would like to see placed within the regular school environment" (1985, p. 525).

Special Case of Distance Education

Distance teaching involves provision of learning programs to "remote" students, generally scattered over a wide geographical area, without the instructor being physically present. Hence, by definition this educational approach must rely on some type of technology to deliver learning materials and assignments and receive responses back from learners. Distance teaching has existed for many decades and has traditionally made heavy use of printed matter (textbooks, study guides, and so on) that are often mailed between the students and educational institution (hence the earlier name of correspondence courses).

Print is certainly a cheap and versatile medium, but it has some important disadvantages—primarily the inherent limitations on instructor-learner interaction. Thus it is not surprising that educators have been very active in exploring alternative technologies that might be used to deliver and enhance distance courses. Radio was used in Australia shortly after the development of public broadcasting in that country. And Smith and Stroud, in the 1982 volume, reviewed a wide range of subsequent communications technologies that have been used for distance instruction.

One set of technologies seeks to expand the range and sophistication of the learning experience available to students—for example, television, which is a much publicized component of programs offered by the British Open University. A second set of technologies has been used to enhance communication between students and the institution. The most common approach is referred to as teleconferencing (usually by audio alone, although video communication is technically possible). A third set of technologies involves the computer, which can be used both for delivery of instruction and as a two- (or multi-) way interactive device.

Technology to Deliver Distance Courses. A number of distance education institutions rely on electronic communication for course delivery. For instance, the National Technological University (NTU) in the United States provides continuing professional education to business and industry via satellite-delivered television courses. Communication is mainly one-way, but there are limited opportunities for students at participating sites to interact with the teacher via an audio link. Some developing countries have looked to mass communication technologies, such as television, to reach large numbers of distance students. For example, the Chinese Open University serves hundreds of thousands of students by relaying television courses to numerous remote sites where groups of learners gather to view the programs. No provision is made for students to interact with the instructor, and a good deal of inconvenience is involved for students, who may have to travel considerable distances to attend the viewing sites. In both the Chinese and NTU examples it is interesting to note that use of modern technology does not necessarily imply pedagogical sophistication.

Technology to Facilitate Human Interaction. Many of the technologies used for delivering instruction to remote learners can also enable students to interact with their teacher and with each other. For example, the underlying idea of videotex was to use an ordinary television set to present text and graphics stored in a central computer. Communication was via telephone lines, and the user could communicate back to the data source by a keypad. Hence, the technology was seen not just as a means of access to information but as a form of CAI. Videotex systems

(Telidon in Canada, Prestel in Britain are examples) enjoyed a brief flurry of interest but have never been commercially successful for delivering instruction. Certainly the rather fanciful scenario sketched out by Syrett in *Expanding Learning Through New Communications Technologies* (in which "Mary Futura" completes undergraduate courses via interactive television) seems unlikely ever to come to fruition. The Telidon field trials project managed by Syrett was abandoned by the Ontario Educational Communications Authority several years ago.

Audioteleconferencing (linking students and instructor by telephone, radio, or satellite) is in wide use in distance education programs, especially where large physical distances are involved (Canada, Australia). Video teleconferencing presents more of a problem due to logistical and cost factors but has been used successfully, especially by the medical profession for continuing education (examples include the Ontario Telehealth and Telemedicine programs, which link hospitals by cable or microwave and allow presentation of medical case studies from any of the participating sites).

Although it is possible to have two-way video, in practice this is rarely done because the expense and equipment involved (for example, satellite up-link) restricts the number of sites available. Much more common is a two-way audio, supplemented by such devices as the electronic blackboard or slow-scan TV, which can be transmitted via ordinary telephone lines. This is the approach adopted, for example, by the University of the West Indies in its UWIDITE distance education program that links remote sites across the Caribbean.

Computers and Distance Education. The use of computers in distance education has excited considerable interest among professionals in the field and was a major theme of the recent conference of the International Council on Distance Education (ICDE) held in Melbourne in 1985. However, review of the ICDE papers presented on this topic indicates that many of the computer applications remain as yet in an experimental stage. Furthermore, there appears to be some uncertainty in the field as to how best this technology might be employed. Some approaches have attempted to use CAI as the principal means of delivering instruction. For example, diskettes are sent out through the mail or courseware is down-loaded electronically from the institution to students' home computers. One obvious snag with such an approach is that many students in distance programs do not own a computer. In any case, given the reservations made earlier about the current state of CAI materials, the notion of using computers as the primary means of delivering course content for distance learners seems questionable.

A much more promising application involves various forms of computer conferencing in which information can be exchanged between students and with the instructor, electronic tutorials can be conducted, assignments can be given, answered, and commented on, reference lists can be distributed, and so on. Students can also use their terminals to gain access to remote data bases relevant to the course and therefore can take a much larger role in directing their own learning. It is not even necessary that individual students own computers as long as they have access to a machine that is capable of being linked with a host site (for example, via telephone lines). A particular advantage of using computers for such interaction is that communication does not have to be in "real time." Instead, messages can be read and answered when it is convenient to the student. This is especially convenient for distance learners who are often studying under severe time constraints.

Impact of Technology on Instructional Practice. Some of the examples cited here appear to hold great promise for overcoming longstanding difficulties involved in distance education—in particular, problems associated with the isolation of the distance learner from the institution and from other students. Despite this potential, however, many of the applications of technology to teaching at a distance have been pedagogically limited or disappointing. Others remain in an experimental stage, supported by special, short-term funding arrangements and not fully integrated with the mainstream programs of the institution.

The principal impetus for distance instruction is that it greatly enhances access to educational opportunity. Hence the technologies of greatest interest in this field are those like television and information technology tht have the potential to extend the "reach" of the institution and teacher. But while this extension may be technologically possible, access can be severely curtailed by other factors such as costs and availability of equipment. In distance education, simple, flexible media generally have the edge over more sophisticated technologies, as Schramm (1977) observed a decade ago. Hence the dominant mode of instruction continues to be print, supplemented by audio cassettes and, increasingly, videocassettes. This is true even for the British Open University, which is renowned for its use of broadcast television. And the distance education program operated by the University of the South Pacific uses its impressive satellite links to the (very) remote sites primarily for administrative functions.

Computer as a Learning Tool

As explained earlier in this chapter, great efforts have been made to find technologies that are educationally self-sufficient and might hence replace teachers as the prime deliverers of instruction. This was the hope for programmed instruction and television and, more recently, was the underlying objective for the development of much CAI. But while computer-assisted instruction has encroached only marginally upon traditional methods of teaching in postsecondary education, other educational uses for computers have begun to transform the way learning takes place in many North American colleges and universities.

Computers were originally developed to help solve tasks that were onerous, complex, and time-consuming. Originally (as the name suggests) these involved processing numbers. More recently, the impetus has shifted to include manipulation of verbal information. Although some diehards find it difficult to accept that such tasks as word processing are really appropriate for computers, in the past few years there has been an enormous interest in using computers as a general-purpose learning tool.

At one time exposure to computers was largely confined to computer science or engineering students who learned programming. Later the computer was used by mathematics and social science students to help with computational and statistical tasks. With the advent of powerful and relatively cheap microcomputers the range of applications has broadened considerably. The most common use is undoubtedly word-processing, which a recent EDUCOM survey (1987) found accounted for over 40 percent of student computing in the postsecondary institutions included in its sample. Various types of data manipulation, using statistical package or spreadsheets, also account for a significant amount of student computing. Use of data bases (say, to compile a bibliography) is a fairly common application, and there are of course a variety of special applications used in teaching specific disciplines, ranging from computer-assisted design to musical composition. It is interesting that, unlike the case with CAI, most of the software was not developed for instructional purposes. In many instances educators have simply used or adapted commercial packages that are widely employed in the professions, with the result that students acquire specialized knowledge or skills as well as computing expertise.

Packages Versus Programming. Most of these applications come in the form of self-contained packages in which students need know little about either programming or the inner logic of the computer. At the same time, some programming is still taught, especially for students in the applied sciences and mathematics. Learning of programming languages—at one time essential to make use of a computer at all—is still claimed by some academics to be a valuable skill in its own right. It is held that the underlying principles of programming can be applied to a variety of other problem-solving situations (similar arguments were made in times past for learning logic and classical languages). Burton (1986) conducted an extensive literature review on the relationship between programming skills and generic problem-solving abilities and found most of the published research methodologically flawed. Despite "encouraging signs" he concluded that "precious little" can be said about the relationship (p. 32).

It seems possible that software developments already in hand may make traditional programming skills largely redundant for many ordinary users. In 1987 Apple introduced a package called Hypercard that allows programs to be written by nonprogrammers—what its author, William Atkinson, calls an erector set that can be used to construct whatever applications the user may need (Lewis, 1987).

Computer Literacy. The increasing use of computers as tools for learning reflects the growing reliance on computers to accomplish a variety of tasks, as society moves inexorably from an industrial age into an information age (Bell, 1967). Some educators have referred to a need for computer literacy to supplement the roster of desirable skills that students should acquire before graduation. Whether or not computer literacy is a meaningful concept (any more than calculator literacy or automobile literacy) and, if so, what skills and knowledge it might comprise, the fact remains that appropriate use of computers will be an important requirement for many professions in the future. Thus it is not surprising that many universities are struggling to find the best ways of exposing students to a range of relevant computer applications.

Student-Owned Computers. One trend that has received a good deal of attention in the past five years is to require students to purchase their own computers for use while at college. Despite considerable publicity given to initiatives at schools such as Drexel and Clarkson, a recent survey by EDUCOM of 211 U.S. higher education institutions found that less than a fifth of them required or highly recommended their students purchase a computer—and for the great majority of schools that did, it was only required in some departments or faculties. Only 13 percent of students at the 211 colleges and universities in fact owned their own machines, although the numbers are much higher if only professional and graduate schools are considered. Furthermore, the number is growing, and those that stipulate purchase are the more prestigious and selective institutions. Perhaps most significant was the fact that over half the schools required a computing course for the students to graduate.

Some Problems. The rapid encroachment of computers into university classrooms (albeit not for the purposes that educators originally envisaged) is not without its problems. For instance, dissatisfaction has been expressed in some quarters about the lack of a suitable machine for educational purposes, and the InterUniversity Consortium for Educational Computing, made up of twenty-six leading U.S. technological universities and launched with a grant of $1 million from the Carnegie Corporation, successfully lobbied computer manufacturers to produce a powerful machine suitable for academic use. IBM, Digital Equipment Corporation, and Apple all now manufacture a desktop computer that meets the consortium's specifications in every respect except price (the requirement was for a machine costing less than $3,000). The next challenge is to produce educational software that will fully exploit the capabilities of the hardware.

While the consortium has focused on technologically sophisticated applications, other educators have been concerned with the other end of the spectrum—students who enter the institution with few or no computing skills. In the less prestigious American universities (and in most institutions in the poorer nations) the major need is simply for access to appropriate equipment and for machines that will facilitate learning by relatively inexperienced students. Tucker (1983–84) has referred to this as "robust computation"—meaning an environment that will stand up to the rough-and-tumble of educational use as well as such familiar learning tools as books and pens.

Still other problems with introducing computers into the curriculum involve such factors as equipment compatibility, provision of appropriate technical support services, and the need to train faculty in appropriate educational applications, bearing in mind that many university teachers lack basic computing skills that are becoming commonplace for today's high school graduates.

Conclusions

Changes in Teaching Practice. As this chapter has demonstrated, educators have not been slow to develop technological applications for the improvement of teaching and learning. But to what extent are these approaches in common use throughout the college and university system? It is difficult to obtain an accurate estimate of the prevalence of technology-based approaches in comparison to traditional classroom teaching in colleges and universities. There is clearly extensive use of technological aids to instruction, such as the overhead projector, but technological substitutes for the human teacher appear to be comparatively rare. Even in the case of distance education, which necessarily relies on technology to communicate with students, the media involved are most likely to be simple, and inexpensive (print, audio cassettes), despite considerable attention devoted to more glamorous technologies, such as television and computer conferencing. This is not to say that nothing has changed since the previous volume appeared. Certainly there have been some technological advances (such as those reviewed above), and to some extent instructional practices have reflected these developments. In higher education it appears that the changes in teaching methods have been modest, while student use of computers as a tool has made considerable strides.

Effectiveness of Technology. A second question involves the effectiveness of those technologies that are being used in higher education. Despite the impression given by some enthusiasts, the use of innovations in education is not an end in itself but merely a means to attain some other worthwhile objective. Whether or not educational technologies are seen as successful depends on the objectives they will help achieve. It is commonly argued that appropriate use of technology will make learning more effective or efficient—for example, by allowing acquisition of information in a shorter time or by reducing instructional costs. A great deal has been written about the relative effectiveness of many of the innovations discussed here, generally in comparison to traditional classroom instruction. Results are equivocal, largely because it is so difficult to rule out extraneous variables and to pin down just what is being compared and according to what criteria. Most of the sophisticated technologies described in this chapter are not cheap: It remains conventional wisdom that it takes from 200 to 300 hours of preparation time to develop an hour of good CAI courseware. It also requires a broad range of expertise. For example, Bork (1985), based on more than twenty years of experience developing courseware, says that a minimum writing team should comprise a subject-matter expert, instructional designer, and programmer—a combination only likely to be found in commercial publishing or software houses.

Certainly students can learn from such technologies as CAI and television. Given the immense human proclivity for learning throughout life and in a variety of situations, it would be amazing if they did not! A good deal of the early studies on educational technology focused on demonstrating that mastery of facts was particularly efficient compared to what is acquired in the traditional classroom. Ironically, however, acquisition of information is becoming an increasingly hopeless (and, to some extent, redundant) task as knowledge continues to explode. In the world of the future it seems likely that storing and management of data will more and more be left to computers themselves.

Instructional Quality and Educational Objectives. Meanwhile much use of technology in education is either still experimental or trivial. Instructional models used by technology-based teaching remain those of the traditional classroom and are for the most part based on a simplistic assumptions about the learning process derived from stimulus-response psychology. The great majority of programs available are drill-and-practice or simple tutorials. In fact, between 1982 and 1984 the proportion of such programs markedly increased, while the percentage of more sophisticated simulation programs fell (Gooler, 1986). Haven (1985), on the basis of reviews of almost 8,000 available commercial software packages, reported that the general quality was "barely adequate" and that most programs failed to take advantage of the computing power available to implement more effective pedagogical strategies. This may well be because programs that fully exploit the capabilities of the machine, meet higher-level instructional objectives, and are pedagogically sophisticated are much more difficult and expensive to develop and put on the market.

It is for such reasons that a number of educational critics have espoused educational aims that emphasize more generic skills of "learning to learn" (see Knapper and Cropley, 1985). They see the main goal of a university education as being to equip students with the motivation and ability to learn throughout their lives in a wide variety of situations. Cropley developed this idea in a chapter written for *Expanding Learning Through New Communications Technologies* and then went on to pose the question of whether technology might help achieve such goals. His conclusions were cautiously optimistic, but he warned that use of technology for its own sake would achieve little of permanent value.

The implication of Cropley's remarks is that technology can sometimes constitute a solution looking for a problem. Lewis (1985) attempted to correct this fault in a series of interviews with college and university faculty. Rather than asking respondents what use they saw for particular educational technologies, he instead enquired about the types of instructional problems they faced and then attempted to examine how technology might provide an answer. Interestingly, there was by no means a perfect match between the perceived educational problems and the most common "solutions" offered in existing educational software. For example, the majority of available CAI material is highly didactic and focuses on mastery of content, whereas a commonly cited educational need was identified as teaching learning processes, especially ones that might be transferred to the "real world."

Another set of possible educational objectives, referred to repeatedly above in the context of distance education, involves broadening access to educational opportunity. This is not simply a matter of reaching remote learners but also involves facilitating learning for special groups who may encounter difficulties with conventional teaching. Examples include the elderly and the physically handicapped. Although technology-based instruction would appear to have considerable potential for such groups, practical applications to date remain very limited. In the technology-rich nations of North America it is easy to forget that in many Third World countries even the most basic educational media, such as books or chalk, may be a luxury. Hence to see information technology as a means of transforming education worldwide and redressing the imbalance between information-rich and information-poor countries is at best an oversimplification, and at worst naive. Indeed, it seems quite plausible that the information age might allow the developed nations to further increase their economic superiority.

This chapter has reviewed a wide range of instructional technologies and distinguished between three broad types of application: technologies as instructional aids, technology-based instructional delivery systems, and technologies as learning tools. Of these, the last two applications have the most profound implications for educational practice. While the greatest efforts have probably been put into devising methods that could supplant the human teacher (for example, the teaching machine, educational television, and CAI), by and large these efforts have proved no more successful in 1987 than they did in 1985 or, for that matter, in 1965. Meanwhile, a quiet revolution has been taking place in society as a whole, in which information has gradually replaced manufactured goods as a basis for prosperity and development. The most powerful agent of this new resource is the computer. Not surprisingly, computers and computing skills have become increasingly common in university classrooms—not as replacements for teachers but as useful devices for learning a wide variety of skills, from word processing to statistical calculation. In this sense, the computer is used as an aid in much the same way as a calculator or typewriter—the difference being in the machine's immense power and versatility. Although the seeds of this development can be traced back to 1981 when *Expanding Learning Through New Communications Technologies* was prepared, progress in the past six years—especially in North America—has been astonishing and has paralleled the explosive growth in the number of microcomputers available in the community at large.

It seems almost certain that this trend will continue over the next decade, with ever more powerful computers becoming cheaply available in the workplace, the home, and the classroom. Similarly, the range of possible applications will continue to grow by leaps and bounds. Based on recent developments, it seems likely that educational uses of technology will continue to increase in parallel with developments in the outside world. If this results—as seems probable—in a greater emphasis on learning skills as opposed to teaching skills, then there will be major implications for the future of instructional practice and for the quality of learning in postsecondary education. For this author at least, such a change to student-centered learning, with an emphasis on generic skill acquisition as opposed to mastering content and facts, would only be to the good.

References

Bell, D. "Notes on the Post-Industrial Society." *Public Interest*, 1967, *6*, 119-130.
Bork, A. "Development of Computer Based Learning Material." Address to NATO Advanced Study Institute, San Miniato, Italy, 1985.
Burton, J. K. "Computer Programming and Generalized Problem Solving Skills: In Search of Direction." Paper presented at the annual meeting of the American Educational Research Association, San Francisco, April 1986.
EDUCOM. *Microcomputer Use in Higher Education*. Washington, D.C.: EDUCOM and *Chronicle of Higher Education*, 1987.

46

Gooler, D. D. *The Education Utility: The Power to Revitalize Education and Society.* Englewood Cliffs, N.J.: Educational Technology Publications, 1986.

Haven, R. "An Analysis of Instructional Trends in Educational Software." Paper presented at the annual meeting of the American Educational Research Association, Chicago, April 1985.

Jones, M. "Applications of Artificial Intelligence Within Education." *International Journal of Computers and Mathematics with Applications,* 1985, *11,* 517–526.

Knapper, C. K. (ed.). *Expanding Learning Through New Communications Technologies.* New Directions for Teaching and Learning, no. 9. San Francisco: Jossey-Bass, 1982.

Knapper, C. K., and Cropley, A. J. *Lifelong Learning and Higher Education.* London: Croom Helm, 1985.

Lewis, B. N. "The Rationale of Adaptive Teaching Machines." In M. Goldsmith (ed.), *Mechanization in the Classroom,* London: Souvenir Press, 1963.

Lewis, P. "Software for Mac Called 'Revolutionary.' " *Toronto Globe and Mail,* Aug. 21, 1987, p. B8.

Lewis, R. J. *Faculty Perspectives on the Role of Information Technologies in Academic Instruction.* Washington, D.C.: Corporation for Public Broadcasting, 1985.

Perkins, D. N. "The Fingertip Effect: How Information-Processing Technology Shapes Thinking." *Educational Researcher,* 1985, *17,* 11–17.

Schramm, W. *Big Media, Little Media: Tools and Technologies for Instruction.* Newbury Park, Calif: Sage, 1977.

Taylor, J. "Courseware Development for Interactive Videodisc: A Case Study." Paper presented at the conference of the International Council on Distance Education, Melbourne, Australia, August 1985.

Tucker, M. S. *Computers on Campus: Working Papers.* Current Issues in Higher Education, no. 2. Washington, D.C.: American Association for Higher Education, 1983–84.

Wheeler, D. L. "Artificial-Intelligence Researchers Develop Electronic 'Tutors' to Aid Learning Process." *Chronicle of Higher Education,* May 20, 1987, pp. 6–8.

Christopher K. Knapper is director of teaching resources and continuing education at the University of Waterloo, Ontario, Canada, where he also serves as professor of environmental studies and psychology. He has written widely on higher education, especially distance education, instructional evaluation, and educational technology. His most recent book, coauthored with Arthur Cropley, is Lifelong Learning and Higher Education.

*Just as students need guidance as learners, professors are
entitled to helpful direction to improve teaching performance.*

Evaluating College Teaching

Peter Seldin

At the heart of every teaching evaluation program is its purpose. Purpose
shapes the kind of questions asked, determines sources of data, fixes the
depth of analysis, and guides the dissemination of evaluation findings.
There are two outstanding purposes for evaluating teaching: first, the
improvement of teaching performance and, second, administrative decision making.

To be consistent with the other contributions to this volume, this
chapter focuses only on evaluation of teaching for the purpose of strengthening performance. (For detailed information on evaluation for administrative decisions, see *Changing Practices in Faculty Evaluation*, Seldin,
1984.)

Let it be said that there is no worthier reason to evaluate teaching
performance than to improve it. College and university professors are
hired with the expectation that they eventually will offer effective instruction for students. The formal and systematic evaluation of college teaching is no more than a logical extension of this expectation. It also is
good administrative practice. Just as students deserve guidance as
learners, professors are entitled to helpful direction in their teaching. No
matter how good a college teacher is in the classroom or laboratory, he or
she can improve. No matter how effective a particular teaching method
is, it can be enhanced.

Some critics of college teaching evaluation argue that we do not

R. E. Young, K. E. Eble (eds.). *College Teaching and Learning: Preparing for New Commitments.*
New Directions for Teaching and Learning, no. 33. San Francisco: Jossey-Bass, Spring 1988.

have the final answer to the question of what constitutes effective teaching. That may be true, but the key ingredients of effective teaching are increasingly well known. In 1988 we have no reason to ignore hundreds of studies that are in general agreement on these characteristics. They include a deep knowledge of the subject, an ability to communicate with and motivate students, enthusiasm for the subject and for teaching, clarity of presentation, and fairness.

Who can identify the presence or absence of these qualities in a college teacher? Students, faculty colleagues, professors themselves, all take part in a shared judgment of the effectiveness of college teaching, and all contribute to its improvement.

Students

The harvesting of students' assessment of teaching might include student testimonials, exit interviews, suggestion boxes, small discussion groups, and alumni questionnaires. In practice, a written questionnaire or rating scale generally serves as the predominant source of student feedback.

Does the use of student ratings automatically result in improved teaching? For most professors, probably not. Seldin (1987) reports that improvement is contingent on three factors: whether the ratings turned up in an appraisal are new to the professor; whether the professor is motivated to improve; and whether the professor knows how to improve.

Student ratings are more likely to produce a salutary effect when discussed with the professor by a sympathetic and knowledgeable colleague or teaching improvement specialist, who can reassure the teacher that any identified problems are neither unusual nor insurmountable and who can offer appropriate counsel on how to make improvements.

In discussions of the subject of student ratings, college faculty members make the argument that the ratings are influenced by factors beyond the instructor's control. What does the most recent research literature show? No consistent relationship seems to exist between student ratings and an instructor's rank, sex, and research productivity (McKeachie, 1979; Aleamoni and Hexner, 1980; Lowman, 1984; Seldin, 1986). Further, little or no relationship has been found between the students' age, year in college, grade point average, academic ability, sex, and their ratings of instructors (Millman, 1981; Braskamp, Brandenburg, and Ory, 1984; Marsh, 1984). And there appears to be no significant link between the amount of work assigned, grading standards, and student ratings (Lowman, 1984). Ratings are marginally higher in discussion classes, classes in the humanities, and small classes (under thirteen students), but the differences are not statistically significant (Braskamp, Brandenburg, and Ory, 1984; Seldin, 1984).

Most important even when significant relationships between extraneous variables and student ratings are obtained, they account for just 12 to 14 percent of the variance between positive and poor ratings (Marsh, 1980; Seldin, 1986).

Guidelines for Using Student Ratings for Improvement Purposes. More than two decades of intense interest in student ratings of instructors have resulted in some general guidelines and strategy suggestions.

1. Ask diagnostic questions that bring out description and evaluation of specific teaching behaviors and specific aspects of the course. Responses to these questions are likely to be more helpful than those to general questions about teaching effectiveness.

2. Include several items in any student rating instrument from each of the following groupings:

- Structure: "The instructor plans class activities in detail"
- Feedback: "Tests and papers are graded and returned promptly"
- Group interaction: "Students discuss each other's ideas"
- Rapport: "The instructor is friendly"
- Work load: "The instructor asks for too much work"
- Impact on students: "My curiosity is stimulated by this instructor."

3. Give student rating results only to the teacher being evaluated and to no one else without the professor's consent.

4. Ask students only those questions that they can actually answer. College students can describe and judge well items that deal with what they have learned in the course, an instructor's ability to communicate with them, how well prepared an instructor was for class, how accessible the instructor was out of class, how clear and challenging the assignments were. Students, on the other hand, are in a difficult position to describe and judge the relevance or up-to-dateness of course content or the subject knowledge of a professor.

5. Encourage professors to comment on their ratings in light of the methods and goals of the course. Ask them to add two or three questions to the rating form that relate to their specific course objectives or teaching methods.

6. Use multiple sources of information. A student rating form should never be used as the sole basis for evaluating teaching effectiveness. It should be supplemented by data from other sources. Options include classroom observation, analysis of audio or videotapes of classroom sessions, self-evaluation, review of instructional materials, long-term follow-up of students' performance, alumni opinions, and student enrollments in elective courses.

7. Be sure that an adequate number of students complete any evaluation form. If less than 75 percent of the registered students participate,

the results may be suspect. Similarly, for courses with fewer than thirteen students, the results may be statistically unreliable.

8. Provide instructors with help in improving their teaching. Change in teaching performance is far more likely if a knowledgeable colleague or teaching improvement specialist helps interpret scores, provides encouragement, and suggests teaching improvement strategies. A colleague who serves as a counselor generally should not also participate in personnel decisions. Openness and trust are essential for a serious examination of teaching strengths and weaknesses.

9. Pay particular attention to students' written comments to openended questions such as: What are the major strengths of the course? How could the instructor improve as a teacher? Braskamp, Brandenberg, and Ory (1984) have suggested a particularly interesting strategy for collecting written student opinions about courses and instructors: Students are asked to write a one-page mock letter to another student who is interested in taking the same course and instructor the following semester. In the letter, students comment on specific aspects of the course and instructor and conclude with a recommendation that others enroll in or avoid the course and/or instructor.

Mid-Semester Student Evaluations. Most typically, student evaluations are carried out at the end of a course and instructors receive the results some weeks later. That means that student feedback is of no help in fine-tuning the course during the term. Some professors, however, gather their own informal student ratings in mid-semester so that areas of student dissatisfaction (and satisfaction) can be addressed in the course's structure or emphasis in the semester's second half.

Knapper (1984) reports on one method of obtaining student feedback as the course progresses. Prior to the middle of the semester, half a class period is set aside for teaching evaluation. Students form groups of five and each group is asked to reach consensus on three questions: (1) Which parts of the course work well? (2) Which parts need to be refined? (3) What specific recommendations can be made to improve the course? Following ten minutes of discussion, a spokesperson for each group reports the groups' conclusions to the entire class. The instructor then presents an outline of proposed changes, or an explanation of why such changes cannot or should not be made. It is difficult for the professor who teaches the class to refrain from explanations or arguments in the face of student comments. For that reason, it may be advisable to have a neutral third party, such as a faculty colleague or teaching assistant, take the chair for these student feedback sessions.

Weimer (1987) reports that some instructors ask directly for student responses: "I'm going to review for the exam next Friday. Write me a note and let me know the topics you'd like to have me cover." This kind of feedback gives the instructor an indication of the content areas students find unclear and feel need further discussion. That is valuable information about one's teaching.

Since student ratings (like all other sources of information on teaching) are inadequate as a sole judge of instructional effectiveness, what role can be played by faculty colleagues?

Faculty Colleagues

Despite the fact that most college teaching still takes place in isolated classrooms, colleague evaluation has become a significant part of any comprehensive assessment of teaching performance. Two approaches are open to colleagues to assess teaching: examination of instructional materials and classroom visitation. Whichever the approach, the frame of reference is mutual trust and respect, fairness, and a genuine interest in improving college teaching.

Evaluating Instructional Materials. Colleagues within a discipline can judge instructional material in the following areas:

- *Course content.* It is consistent with contemporary knowledge of the subject? Are the breadth and depth of coverage appropriate for the course?
- *Readings.* Do they supplement the lecture notes and class discussion?
- *Textbooks and handouts.* Are they appropriate to the course level? Is the material up-to-date?
- *Course syllabus.* Does it adequately outline the sequence of topics to be covered?
- *Assignments.* Do the assignments reflect course objectives?
- *Course objectives.* Do they represent the desired mastery of the subject? Are course objectives clear to the students?
- *Learning approaches.* Are the learning approaches (texts, reading lists, films, assignments, lectures, discussions) suitable to course content and objectives? Is the course well paced?
- *Examinations and grading.* Is the content of exams representative of the course content and objectives? Are exam items clear and well written? Is the distribution of grades appropriate to the level of the course and preparation of the students enrolled?

As for procedure, there typically is a meeting between the faculty colleagues and the instructor prior to examining the teaching materials. The purpose of the meeting is to explore the goals and characteristics of the course, the type of students enrolled in the course, and any special problems or constraints posed by the evaluation. Braskamp, Brandenburg, and Ory (1984), Seldin (1986), and Sorcinelli (1986) believe that another benefit of this meeting may be new insights into teaching for those doing the evaluating. The sharing of materials among faculty members may help clarify standards of teaching and learning and stimulate the exchange of ideas. That is essential for college teaching to be improved.

Evaluating Classroom Teaching. Colleague visits to the classroom can be an effective approach to improve teaching. If the initiative for the visit comes from the instructor, so much the better. The goal of observing classroom instructional behavior is to evaluate the teaching process and its relationship to student learning. Skillful observers focus on the verbal and nonverbal behaviors of both instructor and students in the classroom.

Successful colleague observation is typically a three-part procedure that includes a preobservation conference in which the observer meets with the instructor to review an outline of the class content, procedures, and objectives; an observation for a full class period; and a postobservation conference—within two or three days of the visit—to discuss tentative conclusions and recommendations.

What are some of the characteristics to look for in observing teaching?

- *Instructor knowledge.* Does the instructor demonstrate a breadth and depth of understanding of the subject? Is the material appropriate to the level of the course and students' backgrounds?
- *Method of instruction.* Is the presentation well organized and planned? Is material clearly presented?
- *Instructor-student rapport.* Does the instructor encourage student participation? Demonstrate fair and equitable treatment of all students in the class?
- *Teaching behaviors.* Is the instructor easily heard? Does the instructor achieve effective communication with students?
- *Enthusiasm.* Does the instructor demonstrate enthusiasm for the subject matter? Show signs of enjoying teaching?
- *Overall.* What parts of the teaching seem to particularly enhance the learning process? What suggestions might improve the teaching performance?

A standardized observation form tends to systematize the evaluation. A form should pose specific questions to generate meaningful information. A point-range approach (such as 1-7) is an easy and useful response format, but there should also be sufficient space for open-ended comments.

The recent experience with classroom observation suggests that teaching performance benefits most if colleagues are trained in observation techniques; findings are discussed in an informal, objective, and descriptive manner; and a climate of candor and trust exists among a faculty committed to continuing to improve the quality of college teaching.

Guidelines for Observing Teaching. Colleague observation of teaching is more likely to result in improved instruction if certain guidelines are followed.

1. Employ as observers only those professors with considerable teaching experience and competence. Train them so they know what to look for and how to provide useful description and evaluation of what they observe.

2. Consider colleague observation as but one piece of information on teaching. Merge the results of classroom observation with the results from other data sources, such as student ratings, colleague assessment of instructional materials, and self-assessment to obtain a more complete and accurate picture of an instructor's teaching performance.

3. Remember that mutual trust and respect among colleagues is necessary for open and honest exchange about strengths and weaknesses and possible improvement strategies.

4. Provide information to the instructor that is descriptive rather than evaluative, specific rather than general, responsive to the needs of the instructor, and directed toward behavior that the instructor can do something about.

Self-Evaluation

Many colleges and universities now consider faculty self-evaluation a useful tool in improving teaching performance. When professors engage in searching self-reflection, it opens an awareness that provides the springboard for teaching improvement. However, self-assessment sometimes fails to produce this improvement. Why? Some teachers do not know how to assess their own performance. Others can identify teaching weaknesses but do not know how to move toward improvement. Still others are taken in by the illusion they foster of themselves as superb teachers.

How is self-evaluation used to strengthen teaching? While no single approach has proven itself best, there are three widely used techniques: discussion on teaching effectiveness with faculty colleagues or teaching improvement specialists; comparison of student and self-ratings; audio and video recording.

Discussions of Teaching Effectiveness. Some teaching improvement specialists are convinced that teaching can be enhanced if the instructor confronts his or her most cherished (and unchallenged) assumptions, values, and attitudes. Simply clarifying an instructor's teaching assumptions, for example, may result in improved classroom performance.

One approach to discussing teaching is the in-depth interview in which the instructor is forced to respond to a series of probing questions about his or her teaching. The purpose is to sensitize the instructor as a teacher. The interview is conducted by a trained faculty member and routinely runs one to three hours. Sometimes, instead of a one-on-one interview, a small group of instructors is asked to reflect on each question and discuss each answer. The participants learn that their colleagues share the same doubts and qualms. By sharing, each emerges from the group discussion more aware, more knowledgeable, and more self-confident as a teacher.

Comparison of Student and Self-Ratings. In this approach students and the instructor complete the identical evaluation form. Then the instructor completes the evaluation form again, this time predicting how he or she will be rated by the students. The value of this technique is that it permits ready comparison of the instructor's self-assessment, the students' ratings, and the instructor's prediction of the student ratings. An honest examination of the triad can be valuable to the instructor desiring to improve.

Pambookian (1977) and Seldin (1980) report that student ratings that are far less favorable than the instructor's self-ratings are more likely to lead to improved teaching than the reverse. Marsh (1984) finds that when students and instructors use the same rating form, they generally show agreement both on overall ratings of the instructor and on such dimensions of teaching as organization and stimulation of interest.

Audio and Video Recording. As instructors listen to and watch their taped classroom performance, they become more aware of their teaching strengths and weaknesses. The tape reminds them of important but forgotten details. Some instructors can watch a tape and recognize immediately how to improve their teaching. But most instructors need faculty colleagues or teaching improvement specialists to help analyze their teaching and to suggest modifications. It helps, too, if instructors can compare their performance with models of good teaching. At some institutions, the taping of classes is done by two cameras. One focuses on the instructor, the other on the students. The tapes are then show simultaneously on a split screen and are reviewed by the instructor and a teaching improvement specialist.

Braskamp, Brandenburg, and Ory (1984) believe that instructors can benefit from systematically analyzing what and how they teach. Their reflections on their teaching, which can be both descriptive and judgmental, should encompass a number of topics: courses taught and enrollments; course materials, syllabus, and assignments; course objectives and goals; course outcomes and student learning as measured by examinations and projects; advising responsibilities; involvement in curriculum projects; and efforts to improve their teaching competence. Instructors can rate themselves by writing answers to direct, open-ended questions or on a set of items on a checklist or rating scale. A combination of the two approaches may be best.

Summary and Conclusions

The formal and systematic evaluation of teaching performance is no longer seen as a panacea for the ailments of American higher education, but it can heighten teacher effectiveness and thereby improve the quality of teaching and learning in our colleges and universities. There are still many unanswered questions about the evaluation of teaching. But from the practical experience and the research of the past decade, we have learned some important things.

We know that some professors have negative attitudes toward instructional evaluation. The data make them defensive, even if the results are not so bad (Weimer, 1987).

We know that evaluation of teaching is a complex process, and no single source of data is adequate. The combined appraisals of students, colleagues, audio and videotapes, and the professor's self-assessment are required for a more accurate and complete picture of an instructor's teaching performance (Seldin, 1984).

We know that many professors have legitimate fears that evaluation data gathered for improvement purposes will be abused by misapplication to tenure, promotion, and retention decisions.

We know that many professors find it awkward and uncomfortable to appraise the teaching performance of their peers.

We know that the likelihood of improvement in teaching increases when an instructor can turn to faculty colleagues or instructional improvement specialists to interpret the ratings and discuss specific strategies for improvement.

We know that professors who trust and respect each other are necessary for open and honest exchange about teaching strengths and weaknesses and specific ways to strengthen performance (Braskamp, Brandenburg, and Ory, 1984).

We know that specific and diagnostic questions should be asked on ratings forms when the purpose of evaluation is to improve teaching performance.

We know that ratings forms should include several open-ended questions so that raters can respond to the questions in their own words.

We know that professors must be in control of their own improvement efforts. In practical terms, this means that they should choose the methods of evaluation and the targeted areas for improvement. This is best done in partnership with a teaching improvement specialist.

And, we know that for most professors, good teaching does not just happen. It is the result of hard work throughout their teaching careers. This kind of long-term commitment to instructional excellence deserves to be recognized and rewarded by every college or university.

References

Aleamoni, L. M., and Hexner, P. Z. "A Review of the Research on Student Evaluation and a Report on the Effect of Different Sets of Instructions on Student Course and Instructor Evaluation." *Instructional Science*, 1980, *9*, 67–84.

Braskamp, L. A., Brandenburg, D. C., and Ory, J. C. *Evaluating Teaching Effectiveness: A Practical Guide.* Newbury Park, Calif.: Sage, 1984.

Knapper, C. K. "Changing Course in Midstream." *Instructional Development at Waterloo*, 1984, *18*, 3.

Lowman, J. *Mastering the Techniques of Teaching.* San Francisco: Jossey-Bass, 1984.

McKeachie, W. J. "Student Ratings of Faculty: A Reprise." *Academe*, 1979, *65*, 384–397.

Marsh, H. W. "The Influence of Student, Course, and Instructor Characteristics on Evaluations of University Teaching." *American Educational Research Journal*, 1980, *17*, 219–237.

Marsh, H. W. "Students' Evaluations of University Teaching: Dimensionality, Reliability, Validity, Potential Biases, and Utility." *Journal of Educational Psychology*, 1984, *76*, 707–754.

Millman, J. (ed.). *Handbook of Teacher Evaluation.* Newbury Park, Calif.: Sage, 1981.

Pambookian, H. S. "Feedback to Instructors on Their Teaching to Improve Instruction." Paper presented at the Third International Conference on Improving University Teaching, Newcastle, England, July 1977.

Seldin, P. *Successful Faculty Evaluation Programs.* Crugers, N.Y.: Coventry Press, 1980.

Seldin, P. *Changing Practices in Faculty Evaluation: A Critical Assessment and Recommendations for Improvement.* San Francisco: Jossey-Bass, 1984.

Seldin, P. "Evaluating Teaching Performance." Workshop presented at the University of Maryland, College Park, February 1986.

Seldin, P. "How to Evaluate Teaching Quality." Guest faculty presentation at the College Management Program, Carnegie-Mellon University, Pittsburgh, July 1987.

Sorcinelli, M. D. *Evaluation of Teaching Handbook.* Bloomington: Dean of Faculties Office, University of Indiana, 1986.

Weimer, M. G. "Translating Evaluation Results into Teaching Improvements." *AAHE Bulletin*, April 1987, pp. 8–11.

Peter Seldin is professor of management at Pace University in Pleasantville, New York. He has consulted widely on faculty evaluation. His most recent publication is Changing Practices in Faculty Evaluation: A Critical Assessment and Recommendations for Improvement *(Jossey-Bass, 1984).*

The faculty development movement of the 1970s and 1980s now turns its attention to the recruitment and preparation of the next generation of college teachers.

Faculty Development and the Future of College Teaching

Paul A. Lacey

It is hard to assess the faculty development movement in American higher education in isolation from the complex system in which it is embedded. If higher education is a jigsaw puzzle, made up of some 600,000 full and part-time faculty, 2,100 baccalaureate-degree granting and a host more two-year and graduate-degree granting institutions, representing a multiplicity of educational goals and purposes—general education, specialized studies, career preparation, research, and public service—then faculty development must be at best a cluster of puzzle pieces and at worst a scatter of parts that take their significance from widely different contexts. Even if space permitted a finished puzzle, conflicting accounts of what the picture is supposed to resemble would make one impossible.

We have had a number of recent prescriptive studies that agree only that higher education is in crisis. Some are calls to renew a vision, to reclaim a heritage, or to restore integrity to the curriculum; some are polemics of an imagined golden age, and others are mean-spirited diatribes portraying the faculty as the enemies of teaching. In particular, *American Professors: A National Resource Imperilled* (Bowen and Schuster, 1986) is a sober assessment of the problems and needs of professors now and through the end of the century, and the Carnegie Foundation's *College: The Undergraduate Experience in America* (Boyer 1987) is a humane

R. E. Young, K. E. Eble (eds.). *College Teaching and Learning: Preparing for New Commitments.*
New Directions for Teaching and Learning, no. 33. San Francisco: Jossey-Bass, Spring 1988.

examination of the needs of undergraduate students. Many of these studies propose faculty development efforts as a means to address the problems they have identified, but of course they show little general agreement about what faculty development is or should be. If one believes that higher education needs to break the hegemony of the discipline and the department, or to radically transform the undergraduate curriculum, or to reverse the research-teaching priorities, or to return undergraduate education to the thrilling days of yesteryear, the usual faculty development activities of leaves and sabbaticals, workshops and seminars, or the evaluation of teaching seem merely palliative.

From the beginnings of the modern faculty development movement in the early 1970s, such hopes and fears for higher education have complicated our assessment of faculty development. Many early programs, at least for a time, used traditional faculty development activities to achieve larger transformations of the curriculum, the institution, or the profession. Over these nearly two decades, the critique of faculty development has often been a critique of higher education: Were we merely rearranging deck chairs on the Titanic? Were we to be the advanced guard of a reform movement, or the Old Guard fighting to maintain the privileges of an unresponsive system in the face of revolutionary demands? Were our programs to be shaped by what might be called the Chicken Little School of Analysis, or were we to take our starting point from what faculty perceived to be their needs, as shaped by such forces as institutional ethos, the demands of the profession, and student evaluations of teaching?

With these questions in mind, this chapter attempts a brief review of what is currently under way in faculty development programs to improve undergraduate learning, to identify the issues being addressed in these programs, and to move from the present to an agenda for the future in faculty development.

Faculty Development and Undergraduate Learning

In 1973 Freedman and Sanford painted a bleak picture of what we knew about teaching and the academic culture. They found among academic men and women a pervasive sense of unease, confusion, and lack of professional identity. "Perhaps the clearest evidence that teaching undergraduates is not a true profession," they argued, "is the fact that professors, when they talk shop, almost never discuss their teaching. Nor do they discuss philosophy of education in any abstract way" (Freedman and Sanford, 1973, p. 11). They further found a lack of research on college teaching and on how students learn.

Since then the literature has burgeoned on the developmental needs of both college students and college faculty, on institutional and professional cultures and how they affect how professors teach, on teaching and learning styles, and on means to assess and evaluate student learning and teaching effectiveness. Books on college teaching have become increasingly research-based and focused on practical issues. National centers on teaching and learning have been created. The most recently founded, the National Center for Research to Improve Postsecondary Teaching and Learning, at the end of just its first year, published ten working papers and reviews of research on such topics as "Approaches to Research on the Improvement of Postsecondary Teaching and Learning" (Green and Stark, 1986), "Postsecondary Teaching and Learning Issues in Search of Researchers" (Vogel and Stark, 1986), and *Teaching and Learning in the College Classroom: A Review of the Research Literature* (McKeachie, Pintrich, Lin, and Smith, 1986). *Faculty as a Key Resource: A Review of the Research Literature* (Blackburn and others, 1987), its review of the faculty development literature, cites over two hundred previous works.

Journals on teaching in specific disciplines offer us accounts of what works in the classroom, and we have had a steady stream of descriptive and analytical studies of a variety of faculty development programs, from the Association of American Colleges (AAC)–sponsored evaluation of programs at twenty colleges and universities, most of them supported by Mellon Foundation funds (Nelsen and Siegel, 1980), to the more recent evaluation of twenty-four programs supported by the Bush Foundation (Eble and McKeachie, 1985) and the report on sources of faculty professional vitality in colleges in the Great Lakes Colleges Association (Brakeman, forthcoming).

We have had descriptions of comprehensive faculty development programs at large universities (Schwen and Sorcinelli, 1983) and particular projects in small colleges and consortia (Nelsen and Siegel, 1980) describing approaches that have worked in a local situation such as small grants, teaching workshops for junior faculty, and evaluation programs for tenured faculty. Foundations have conducted continuing evaluations of major programs, for example, the Lilly Foundation's national Post-Doctoral Teaching Fellows Program and Faculty Open Fellowships Program for faculty from Indiana institutions. Jossey-Bass's *New Directions* series has also provided descriptions of successful programs in faculty development, assessment and improvement of teaching, student services, and instructional and curricular development. The consequence of all this activity is that as a college teaching profession, we talk about some things with more assurance than we did in the past and our shoptalk is now very substantially concerned with teaching and learning.

Consider some of the indicators: When the recent Carnegie study asked students to appraise their teachers and the teaching they received, 71 percent agreed with the statement "overall, I am satisfied with the teaching I have received," 75 percent agreed that "on the whole I trust the faculty here to look out for students' interests," and 81 percent agreed with the statement "most of my professors encourage students to actively participate in class discussion." When asked to respond to the statement "I feel a sense of community at this institution," 61 percent from all institutions agreed, with an agreement rate of 80 percent from liberal arts colleges (Boyer, 1987). Other studies also indicate that a majority of students assess their teachers quite favorably. Blackburn, Boberg, O'Connell, and Pellino (1980) found that students place 90 percent of their faculty in the above average or superior category. Students, by and large, are satisfied with their undergraduate educations.

Faculty Development and Faculty Life

What about faculty members? Eble and McKeachie (1985) remind us that, in a 1978 survey of twenty-three occupations, professors ranked at or close to the top in terms of job satisfaction, freedom from boredom, freedom from irritation, and enjoyment of good health. Faculty members value independence and autonomy, and though they work the most hours of any of the twenty-three occupations (Caplan and others, 1980), Clark (1985) notes that academic employment gives one far more discretionary time, "maneuvering time" than nearly any other profession. The benefits of the profession go a long way to balancing out such detriments as eroding incomes, severely limited professional mobility, poorer quality of campus life, and a reward system that values published research of any quality far above superior teaching (Bowen and Schuster, 1986; Boyer, 1987; Clark, 1985). There are indications, then, that most American college faculty members are generally satisfied with their situations.

Yet, despite the considerable appeal of the instrinsic rewards of teaching (Clark, 1985; McKeachie, 1982), there is a great deal of evidence of job-related stress affecting faculty life. Gmelch, Lovrich, and Wilke (1984) uncovered six sources of stress, identified by 40 percent or more of the respondents:

1. Imposing excessively high self-expectations   53%
2. Securing financial support for my research   50%
3. Having sufficient time to keep abreast of current developments in my field   49%
4. Receiving inadequate salary to meet financial needs   41%
5. Preparing a manuscript for publication   40%
6. Feeling that I have too heavy a work load, one that I cannot possibly finish during the normal work day.   40%

Five of the ten most cited stressors relate to time or resource constraints. Excessively high self-imposed expectations also appear in one form or another among several of the sources of stress. Ambiguity over the criteria that are used to evaluate faculty in the areas of teaching and research also seem to be a major contributor to faculty stress (Gmelch, Lovrich, and Wilke, 1984).

Bowen and Schuster (1986) report that 90 percent of the faculty they surveyed would choose the same profession again, yet they go on to describe professors as "dispirited, fragmented, devalued and dedicated" and describe the American professoriate as a "resource imperilled." Boyer (1987) reports that 41 percent of the Carnegie study sample are less enthusiastic about their work now than when they began their careers, about half say they would consider another academic job if it were offered them, and 46 percent say they would consider a nonacademic job if one came along. A particular source of discordance is the tug between the teaching and research expectations of American colleges and universities. Sixty-three percent of the faculty surveyed said that their interests "lie toward teaching as opposed to research," and even at research universities almost 40 percent of the faculty showed a strong preference for teaching. That confirms similar findings, notably Ladd (1979), that faculty think of themselves primarily as teachers, not researchers, and that the bulk of published research is undertaken by only a small percentage of university and college faculty. Bowen and Schuster (1986) and Boyer (1987) join a line of studies that show that research is more highly rewarded than teaching and that faculty see these two activities as in direct competition for time and attention. While Boyer finds the condition of teaching a pattern of contradictions, perhaps the most glaring being that many faculty prefer teaching to research and may "endure personal discontentment about the conflict," the AAC report sneers, "Adept at looking out for themselves . . . professors unquestionably offer in their courses exquisite examples of specialized learning. But who looks after the shop? . . . The language of the Academy is revealing: professors speak of teaching *loads* and research *opportunities*, never the reverse" (Curtis and others, 1985).

We know some of the key issues to be addressed by faculty development activities: how to structure learning and assessment situations to maximize student learning; how to enhance the intrinsic satisfactions in teaching, how to encourage and energize faculty to strengthen their teaching; how to work to overcome problems of extreme stress, low morale, and burnout; how to meet the divergent needs of junior and senior faculty so that greater mutual support and collegiality might result; how to integrate teaching and research so that they are mutually supportive; and how to enhance teaching in a system that rewards research more highly. In isolation, some of those look relatively easy to address. The central qualities of good teaching, Boyer (1987) tells us, are generally agreed on: command of material, staying abreast of the field and skillfully communicating information to students, contagious enthusiasm for the play of ideas, optimism about human potential, involving one's students, sensitivity, integrity, and warmth as a human being. Developing those skills and personal qualities under the stress cited above, however, is the challenge that faculty development faces.

Faculty Development Programs

Blackburn and others (1987) tell us that a great deal is known about how faculty spend their time, the amount they give to teaching, how much they produce in the way of articles, what they have as goals for undergraduates, how they are rated by students, and the like. "What we did not find . . . were studies from the faculty member's perspective. . . . How professors deal with: a bad class, the stress they feel, a nonsupportive environment, poorly-prepared students, frustration, alienation—the concerns we were hearing about in our interviews" (Blackburn and others, 1987, p. 25). These are matters not only for research but also for attention in faculty development programs. Which of them is addressed and how should be the subject of any assessment of where the faculty development movement is going.

Fortunately, several recent studies throw light on these and related questions. The Professional and Organizational Development (POD) Network "Survey of Faculty Development Practices" (Erickson, 1986) brings us up-to-date on what is being done nationally in the name of faculty development; *Improving Undergraduate Education Through Faculty Development* (Eble and McKeachie, 1985) offers an evaluation of twenty-four Bush Foundation–supported programs, and Brakeman (forthcoming) discusses how the interplay of a variety of activities and influences serve to vitalize the faculty of twelve liberal arts colleges.

It has been widely believed that faculty development programs were in a decline due to widespread budget constraints. Of seventy-two faculty development centers listed by Gaff in 1975, 28 percent had closed by 1984 (Gustafson and Bratton, 1984). Erickson (1986), however, paints a different picture. Forty-four percent of four-year institutions reported some significant formal structure for faculty development or instructional improvement, and 66 percent of the respondents reported that their institution's current investment in faculty instructional and professional development was much or somewhat greater than it had been three years earlier. Though some programs have closed or been curtailed, more are starting up than are closing. The POD study concludes that "probably half or more of our four-year colleges, universities and professional schools offer some formal faculty development, instructional development, and/or teaching improvement services" (Erickson, 1986).

Both the range of resources and services available and the articulation of offerings to assess and strengthen teaching effectiveness are noteworthy. Again using the POD data (Erickson, 1986), more than 96 percent of the institutions used student ratings of instruction; more than 64 percent had classroom observation by peers; over half had peer review of course materials; around half provided consultation on teaching from trained colleagues or other instructional resource people and videotaping and critique of classroom instruction. Though individual help for faculty is less frequent, more than a third of the institutions have such help for interpreting student ratings, for course planning or development, and for developing teaching skills; over half provide such consultation for use of instructional technology. Around one-quarter of the institutions have a program of professional and personal "growth contract" plans for faculty, and over 70 percent have periodic review for all faculty, including tenured faculty.

Perhaps more impressive is how workshops or seminars and grants and leaves are focused on strengthening teaching. Workshops or seminars on methods or techniques of instruction are offered by over 60 percent of the institutions, on course or curricular planning by over one-third, on testing and evaluating student performance by one-third, and on academic and advising skills by over half. Over 60 percent of the institutions report programs of grants for faculty developing new or different approaches to course or teaching; 60 percent provide summer grants for instructional improvement projects; over 50 percent provide for temporary load reductions for faculty to work on new course, major course revision, or research area; about 20 percent provide a lower than normal teaching load for first-year faculty. Given the strong pressures and incentives to put grant and leave resources into traditional sabbatical support for research and travel funds into research and attending conferences, this degree of support for teaching and instructional and curricular development speaks to the seriousness with which activities focused on improving teaching and learning are being pursued.

The POD Network survey does not attempt to assess the quality of these activities or to determine how many faculty members participate in any of them, but the overview gives credibility to the descriptions of seminars, instructional development approaches, teaching review activities, and other projects that particular institutions have reported in the growing faculty development literature, particularly those reports that emphasize improved morale and collegiality resulting from the activities. To the extent that numbers alone can tell us anything, we can conclude that substantial resources and effort are being given to assessing and improving teaching in American colleges and universities.

Characteristics of Successful Programs

The twenty-four faculty development programs studied by Eble and McKeachie (1985) differed from one another as widely as did the institutions—small- to medium-sized private colleges, large public universities, church-related colleges, highly selective independent colleges. Each designed a program it perceived to meet its own needs; consequently, some programs were single focus, usually individual grants to support research and publication; some offered a "cafeteria" of activities seeking to address as many institutional hopes and needs as possible; and some concentrated on a limited number of connected purposes. The Bush Foundation offered planning grants and staff consultation to the institutions, so most program designs reflect a careful assessment of needs in relation to each institution's ethos. Grants were made for three-year periods, with the possibility of a renewal for three more years.

Among the fourteen common characteristics Eble and McKeachie identify in the most successful programs, there are some that seem consistent with the growing experience in faculty development. The programs were carefully planned and were neither too limited nor too broad but offered a diversity of opportunities to meet faculty needs. The program maintained an identity, involved faculty and administration in leadership so that faculty felt ownership of the program but broader institutional needs were also served, created situations in which faculty felt increased colleague support for investments in teaching and a greater sense that administrators valued teaching, stimulated faculty enthusiasm and participation, had high visibility on campus, and provided training to develop new skills. It offered activities that resulted in tangible changes in courses, teaching strategies, subject matter competence, and curricula, and that increased interaction and communication among faculty and students in working toward common goals.

These characteristics point to some important lessons learned for faculty development programs. We know that faculty members' most preferred form of development support is individual grants for study and research. Programs that disburse money that way—as some of the Bush programs did—undoubtedly please the recipients, and this may have some marginal effect in the classroom because teachers are happy with their professional lives and somewhat refreshed by their time away from teaching. Personal and institutional reputations may be enhanced. Though it is an article of faith in the profession that research, even in the most specialized areas, makes for better teaching, the evidence is hardly even anecdotal; people just say so.

Workshops and seminars, the most common offering of faculty development programs, have frequently received low ratings for effectiveness, but Eble and McKeachie (1985) found that these have been more highly valued in the Bush programs. This may be a further indication of the importance of careful planning; workshops on new methods of instruction, using computers in teaching, teaching writing across the curriculum, for example, are popular and effective because they address practical needs and can result in tangible changes in the way faculty teach. Activities that attempted to address very broad questions on liberal education, on the other hand, did not sustain student and faculty enthusiasm. Some of the most valuable reported outcomes of successful workshops or seminars have to do with increased collegiality and better communication among faculty, but the Bush programs bear out what many have learned in faculty development programs over the years: Increased collegiality comes as a by-product of working on matters of importance to us as teachers and professionals.

A mix of individual and group activities, individual grants tied to meeting institutional needs, developing interdisciplinary courses or linking actual research to actual teaching, activities that work in harmony with the actual values of the institution—these seem to be some of the key components of successful faculty development programs. The least successful programs, as Eble and McKeachie identified them, were well planned and executed, but they served limited or routine interests of faculty and administration, lacked a sense of purpose related to enhancing teaching, failed to arouse enthusiasm or produce leadership in faculty or administration, and failed to propose appropriate or effective strategies to meet specific problems.

Finally, Brakeman's (forthcoming) study of faculties of twelve colleges in a consortium that has actively engaged in faculty development programs since 1974, while still in progress, offers support to the Eble and McKeachie conclusions about successful faculty development programs. Brakeman asked faculty to report three subjects: what faculty development activities they engaged in, what activities have contributed most to their professional growth as teachers and scholars, and what has been good about teaching at their colleges. The interplay in the responses to these three questions is especially interesting. The seven professional activities most frequently engaged in were, in rank order, professional meetings (96 percent), sabbaticals or leaves (78 percent), summer money from college (63 percent), consortial conferences or workshops (54 percent), research money from other sources (50 percent), nonconsortial workshops (48 percent), and professional consulting (46 percent). Internships, off-campus study programs, consortium summer programs, service on consortium committees, or working for professional organizations were all mentioned by substantial numbers of people.

When asked to identify what has contributed most to professional growth as a teacher and scholar, 25 percent of Brakeman's respondents cited teaching, 34 percent cited research, 22 percent cited leaves, and 17 percent cited local colleagues. When asked to identify what has been good about teaching at the individual's college, 79 percent cited teaching itself, 69 percent cited research, 66 percent cited leaves, and 81 percent cited local colleagues.

These responses indicate that faculty see a high degree of congruence in what contributes to their professional growth and what has been good about teaching in their experience. These are people deeply invested in professional associations, giving papers, doing research, and publishing, but they are also engaged in a wide range of workshop and conference opportunities beyond their discipline; they find ways to grow off-campus, through consulting, off-campus study programs, internships, and other work opportunities. Furthermore, if "professional growth" is taken to mean accomplishment in research and publication, and standing in one's discipline, it can be expected that research itself would be cited most frequently. It is all the more telling, then, that about one-third of these respondents cited research and one-quarter cited teaching as contributing most to their professional growth. Furthermore, local colleagues would seem to play an unexpectedly large part in professional growth, given that small college faculties rarely offer the opportunity to work next to other members of one's subdisciplines. Colleagues, the teaching itself, and research have almost equal impact on good teaching in these colleges.

Clearly, these highlights of a complex study still under way are more suggestive than conclusive. Nonetheless, they add support to the model of successful faculty development activities that Eble and McKeachie (1985) develop from their study of the Bush programs. That model suggests a two-pronged approach to faculty development. It argues that "individual change will be most successful and enduring when it enhances faculty members' intrinsic satisfactions in teaching, that is, when it contributes to feelings of self-competence, achievement, mastery, autonomy, intellectual curiosity, and engagement" (p. 50). But change at the individual level is greatly influenced by a sense of social support. Increased communication, raising the norms about teaching, and an enlarged sense of participation are important at the institutional level and in reinforcing and augmenting individual change. Faculty development activities that create or enhance intrinsic motivations to teach well, and that draw significantly on institutional structures that encourage autonomy, independence, and personal initiative, will have the greatest prospect of success, Eble and McKeachie propose.

Developing the Next Generation of College Teachers

This "theory" of faculty development has great power for shaping and assessing future faculty development programs. It also has a great deal to offer us as we begin to address the opportunity to recruit the next generation of college teachers. Bowen and Schuster (1986) estimate that about half a million new faculty members will be needed in American higher education by the next century. Those of us who came into teaching in the boom years—the Korea-generation G.I.'s, the recipients of National Science Foundation, National Defense Act, Danforth, Kent and Wilson Fellowships—are now the largest age-cohort in higher education; our replacements are at present enrolled in our undergraduate courses. Foundations are once again beginning to offer fellowships for college teaching; the Mellon Foundation has reinvented the Woodrow Wilson Fellowships of a generation ago, and the Ford Foundation has begun to fund programs in undergraduate institutions for faculty to work with students who might be encouraged to go into college teaching. What we see before us is an unparalleled opportunity to establish new priorities, especially with reference to the interplay of teaching and research, to enhance teaching quality and the respect of which it is held. And, if it is true that senior faculty, as they look to the end of their careers, tend to shift their own priorities and give greater attention to teaching (Baldwin, 1979; Rice, 1983; Blackburn and others, 1987), we can imagine ways of encouraging and vitalizing the faculty in the very process of recruiting the next generation of teachers. This is an unparalleled opportunity precisely because this time, as opposed to a quarter of a century ago, we have a vast body of research on teaching and learning, and a profession that does talk about teaching and is increasingly reflective about it. And, perhaps most importantly, we have an awareness of the inadequacy of graduate school education for the training of undergraduate teachers.

The last time, foundations were content to give fellowships and let the graduate schools set the norms; one result was that the scholar-teacher model was replaced by the researcher model, an inadequate model, as the surveys indicate, for what we in fact do as college teachers (Rice, 1983). We need not repeat that mistake. Faculty development programs that deliberately apply the Eble and McKeachie model may find ways to strengthen collegiality across age lines, to raise the norms of teaching, to raise the level of shoptalk about teaching, to enable undergraduates to become a richer resource for faculty development activities, and to create better ways to integrate teaching and scholarly activities.

The faculty development movement is alive and as well as can be expected. This movement continues to be a source of health for a higher education system that many critics describe as in crisis. Given the right kind of support, it not only has something to offer the present generation of faculty and students, but it could be a powerful resource for recruiting the next generation of college teachers and, in the process, for raising our expectations for undergraduate teaching.

References

Baldwin, R. "Adult and Career Development: What Are the Implications for Faculty?" *Current Issues in Higher Education*, 1979, 2, 13–20.

68

Blackburn, R. T., Boberg, A., O'Connell, C., and Pellino, G. *Project for Faculty Development Program Evaluation.* Ann Arbor: Center for the Study of Higher Education, University of Michigan, 1980.

Blackburn, R. T., Lawrence, J. H., Ross, S., Okoloko, V., Meiland, R., Bieber, J. P., and Street, T. *Faculty as a Key Resource: A Review of the Research Literature.* Ann Arbor: National Center for Research to Improve Postsecondary Teaching and Learning, University of Michigan, 1987.

Bowen, H., and Schuster, J. *American Professors: A National Resource Imperilled.* Oxford, England: Oxford University Press, 1986.

Boyer, E. L. *College: The Undergraduate Experience in America.* New York: Harper & Row, 1987.

Brakeman, L. F. *We Asked Them: A Report on the Sources of Faculty Professional Vitality in the Great Lakes Colleges Association.* Ann Arbor, Mich.: Great Lakes Colleges Association, forthcoming.

Caplan, R. D., and others. *Job Demands and Worker Health.* Ann Arbor: Institute for Social Research, University of Michigan, 1980.

Centra, J. A. *Determining Faculty Effectiveness: Assessing Teaching, Research, and Service for Personnel Decisions and Improvement.* San Francisco: Jossey-Bass, 1979.

Clark, B. R. "Academic Life in America." *Change Magazine,* September/October 1985, pp. 36–43.

Curtis, M. H., and others. "Integrity in the College Classroom: A Report to the Academic Community." Washington, D.C.: Association of American Colleges, 1985.

Eble, K. E., and McKeachie, W. J. *Improving Undergraduate Education Through Faculty Development: An Analysis of Effective Programs and Practices.* San Francisco: Jossey-Bass, 1985.

Erickson, G. "A Survey of Faculty Development Practices." In M. Svinichi, J. Kurfiss, and J. Stone (eds.), *To Improve the Academy.* Vol. 5. Stillwater, Okla.: Professional and Organizational Development Network in Higher Education and the National Council for Staff, Program, and Organizational Development, 1986.

Freedman, M., and Sanford, N. "The Faculty Member Yesterday and Today." In M. Freedman (ed.), *Facilitating Faculty Development.* New Directions for Higher Education, no. 1. San Francisco: Jossey-Bass, 1973.

Gaff, J. G. *Toward Faculty Renewal: Advances in Faculty, Instructional, and Organizational Development.* San Francisco: Jossey-Bass, 1975.

Gmelch, W. H., Lovrich, N. P., and Wilke, P. K. "Sources of Stress in Academe: A National Perspective." *Research in Higher Education,* 1984, *20* (4), 477–490.

Green, P. J., and Stark, J. S. "Approaches to Research on the Improvement of Postsecondary Teaching and Learning: A Working Paper." Ann Arbor, Mich.: National Center for Research to Improve Postsecondary Teaching and Learning, 1986.

Gustafson, K., and Bratton, B. "Instructional Improvement Centers in Higher Education." *Journal of Instructional Development,* 1984, 7 (2), 2–7.

Ladd, E. C. "Work Experience of American College Professors." In *Current Issues in Higher Education.* Vol. 2. Washington, D.C.: American Association for Higher Education, 1979.

McKeachie, W. J. "The Rewards of Teaching." In J. L. Bess (ed.), *Motivating Professors to Teach Effectively.* New Directions for Teaching and Learning, no. 10. San Francisco: Jossey-Bass, 1982.

69

McKeachie, W. J., Pintrich, P. R., Lin, Y. G., and Smith, D. F. *Teaching and Learning in the College Classroom: A Review of the Research Literature.* Ann Arbor: National Center for Research to Improve Postsecondary Teaching and Learning, University of Michigan, 1986.

Nelsen, W. C., and Siegel, M. S. (eds.). *Effective Approaches to Faculty Development.* Washington, D.C.: Association of American Colleges, 1980.

Rice, R. E. "Being Professional Academically." In D. T. Bedsole (ed.), *Critical Aspects of Faculty Development Programs.* Sherman, Tex.: Center for Program and Institutional Renewal, Austin College, 1983.

Schwen, T. M., and Sorcinelli, M. D. "A Profile of a Postdoctoral Teaching Program." In P. A. Lacey (ed.), *Revitalizing Teaching Through Faculty Development.* New Directions in Teaching and Learning, no. 15. San Francisco: Jossey-Bass, 1983.

Seldin, P. (ed.). *Coping with Faculty Stress.* New Directions for Teaching and Learning, no. 29. San Francisco: Jossey-Bass, 1987.

Vogel, C. D., and Stark, J. S. "Postsecondary Teaching and Learning Issues in Search of Researchers: A Working Paper." Ann Arbor: National Center for Research to Improve Postsecondary Teaching and Learning, University of Michigan, 1986.

Paul A. Lacey is professor of English at Earlham College in Richmond, Indiana.

The most recent research on college-level learning may offer new ways to conceive of college teaching.

Student Learning and College Teaching

Paul R. Pintrich

Research on student learning and cognition in the college classroom has become a "hot" topic in postsecondary education since the publication of *Learning, Cognition, and College Teaching* (McKeachie, 1980). Students, faculty, and administrators have all become concerned with students' learning in the college classroom. In particular, a variety of national reports and popular books (Bok, 1986; Boyer, 1987; National Institute of Education [NIE] Study Group, 1984) have stressed the importance of teaching critical thinking and problem-solving skills to college students. Although this attention to student learning and cognition is encouraging, the current research still emphasizes the same three themes noted by McKeachie (1980) in his introduction to the second volume on teaching and learning.

The first theme was the importance of a general cognitive view of student learning. This approach assumes that the cognitive processes students engage in as they study, listen to lectures, perform lab experiments, participate in discussions, write papers, and take exams are important mediators of what they will learn from these different college tasks. One implication of this view is that while instructors can design tasks to facilitate student learning, students are ultimately responsible for their own learning (McKeachie, Pintrich, Lin, and Smith, 1986). This general

R. E. Young, K. E. Eble (eds.). *College Teaching and Learning: Preparing for New Commitments.*
New Directions for Teaching and Learning, no. 33. San Francisco: Jossey-Bass, Spring 1988.

student mediation or student cognition model has become an important paradigm in the research in elementary and secondary education, supplanting to some degree the traditional process-product paradigm used by many educational researchers in the 1970s (Shulman, 1986). Much of the current research on student learning in the college classroom is in line with this model of student mediation and attempts to analyze in detail the different cognitive aspects of student learning.

Secondly, as might be expected from research that focuses on the detailed analysis of the student as an information processor, the current research is still more descriptive and less prescriptive than older theories of learning. The research on student learning and cognition provides college teachers with fairly accurate and detailed descriptions of how students process information, solve problems, think, and reason, but it does not yet provide teachers with detailed prescriptions for action. In fact, many college faculty would probably have difficulty translating some of the current research on student learning and cognition into directly applicable information relevant to their classroom practice. As Young (1987) has pointed out, there is a need for translators, individuals who can synthesize the current research and develop practical programs or materials that can be readily used by college faculty members to improve instruction.

The third theme concerns the consistent finding that students can differ from one another in the ways they process and think about material to be learned. Individual differences in students' knowledge, cognitive skills, and motivation all influence how and what students learn in college classrooms (Corno and Snow, 1986; Snow and Peterson, 1980). This student attribute perspective or attribute-treatment interaction (ATI) view often has focused on such student personality variables as independence-dependence or reflectivity-impulsivity that are assumed to be relatively stable personality traits of the individual student. More recently, however, ATI research has focused on cognitive and motivational characteristics of students that are assumed to mediate student performance on academic tasks but may not be stable personality traits. For example, students' beliefs about their ability to perform a task—that is, self-efficacy—has been shown to influence their achievement (Schunk, 1985), but a student's self-efficacy can vary by the type of task (multiple-choice exam, essay exam, or term paper) as well as by the content domain (biology, psychology, or English composition). This move away from the view that individual differences are functions of stable personality characteristics to a more social-cognitive view that assumes individual differences are a function of both the student and the situation or task represents a more sophisticated view of attribute-treatment interactions, but it also increases the complexity of the research problem and limits generalizations for practice (Cantor and Kihlstrom, 1987).

Although there are many terms, definitions, and models used to describe these different cognitive aspects of student learning, three general areas of interest to college teachers are the focus of this paper: (1) students' knowledge, (2) students' learning strategies, and (3) students' critical thinking. This chapter briefly describes some of the recent developments in these three areas, illustrating the three themes that still characterize current research on student learning and cognition in the college classroom.

Research on Students' Knowledge

One of the most consistent and powerful findings from recent research on student cognition is that students' prior knowledge of the subject matter exerts a great influence on what students will learn from new material (Anderson, 1985; Gagne, 1985). For example, studies of "experts" and "novices" in reading, mathematics, physics, computer programming, and social studies have shown that the superior performance of the experts is due to both the quantity and organization of their knowledge in the subject area (Bransford, Sherwood, Vye, and Rieser, 1986). This knowledge is assumed to be organized into cognitive representations or structures that guide students' information processing of new material in terms of what they pay attention to, what they encode, and how they organize and connect the new material to their prior knowledge (Corno and Mandinach, 1983; McKeachie, Pintrich, Lin, and Smith, 1986; Weinstein and Mayer, 1986). These knowledge structures or representations are based on what content is presented by the instructor and the texts used in the course, but the model assumes that students actively create their own structure. Accordingly, students' representations of course content can vary widely depending on the students' prior knowledge and experience and are not necessarily simple duplications of the instructors' representation of the course content.

This research on student knowledge has several important implications for college learning and teaching. First, a focus on student knowledge at the college level suggests that instructors need to consider how students' organization of course knowledge is related to performance in class. For example, Naveh-Benjamin, McKeachie, Lin, and Tucker (1986) found that college students' knowledge structures were correlated with achievement on the final exam in the course and final course grade. Two aspects of students' knowledge structure were particularly important: the amount of organization and the similarity to the instructor's organization. Students with more organized knowledge structures did better in the course as long as their structure was similar to the instructor's representation of the course content. On the other hand, for students with low levels of organization, similarity to the instructor's knowledge structure did not seem to matter in terms of performance. These students seem to lack the necessary condition for being similar to the instructor, that is, a well-organized structure (Naveh-Benjamin, McKeachie, Lin, and Tucker, 1986). These results suggest that it is not just how students organize course content, but how the organization reflects an "experts" view—that is, the instructor's view of the content—that influences students' learning in a college course.

This same line of research showed that students' knowledge structures for course material develop over a fourteen-week semester. In comparison to structures at the beginning of the course, students' structures were more organized and similar to the instructor's at the end of the course. In addition, students who received A's or B's in the class showed more development in their structures, while students who failed the course showed very little change in organization or similarity (Naveh-Benjamin, McKeachie, Lin, and Tucker, 1986). This suggests that poor students, who had basically the same structures as good students at the beginning of the course, do not develop appropriate representations of the course content, and this limits their ability to assimilate and learn the new information presented in the course.

Although the study of Naveh-Benjamin, McKeachie, Lin, and Tucker (1986) took place in an undergraduate psychology class at a major research university, recent work funded by the Office of Educational Research and Improvement (OERI) at the National Center for Research to Improve Postsecondary Teaching and Learning (NCRIPTAL) at the University of Michigan (McKeachie, Pintrinch, Lin, and Smith, 1986; Naveh-Benjamin and Lin, 1987) has expanded this line of inquiry to English, biology, and sociology courses from several different types of institutions—a community college, a four-year comprehensive university, and a small liberal arts college. This new work suggests that students' knowledge structures can play an important role in students' learning in courses other than psychology. In addition, preliminary work by Naveh-Benjamin and Lin (1987) on the explicit teaching of the instructors' knowledge structures for the course content shows that these structures can be taught and that this knowledge facilitates students' learning of the course material.

In summary, the research on students' knowledge provides a good description of how cognitive characteristics of students can play an important role in what students learn from a college course. This research does not provide any explicit prescriptions for how to teach a particular content, but it does suggest that students will benefit from having explicit discussion of or direct instruction in how the instructor represents the course material. Future research in this area needs to examine more carefully just how students acquire and assemble these cognitive structures across a variety of college courses as well as the flexibility or adaptiveness of these structures for different domains.

Research on Students' Learning Strategies

The research on students' learning strategies attempts to explain how students acquire and modify their knowledge base. In contrast to the research on knowledge structures, which focuses on domain-specific aspects of student learning, the research on learning strategies attempts to describe the general cognitive processes that students use to learn, remember, and understand the course material (Brown, Bransford, Ferrara, and Campione, 1983; Levin, 1986; Weinstein and Mayer, 1986). This research assumes that students are active learners and that their knowledge about cognitive strategies as well as their actual use of the strategies will influence their learning.

This distinction between students' knowledge of strategies and use of strategies underlies both theoretical and practical issues in research on learning strategies. First, at a theoretical level, there are several different types of knowledge about strategies. Paris, Lipson, and Wixson (1983) have discussed three general types: Declarative, procedural, and conditional. Declarative knowledge refers to students' knowledge about the content or what of strategies. For example, students can know that summarizing the main ideas in a textbook chapter is a useful strategy that should improve performance. Procedural knowledge refers to students' knowledge about how to perform these strategies. For example, they may know that summarizing is a good strategy but not really know to select the main ideas very well. The last type of knowledge, conditional knowledge, describes students' knowledge about when and why to use different learning strategies. For example, students may know what summarizing is and even how to summarize properly, but they also need to know when and why it might be an appropriate strategy, depending on how they will be tested on the textbook chapter. Summarizing may be more important for an essay test where the student has to integrate ideas from various sources; in comparison, on a multiple-choice test that stresses details and facts it may be more advantageous to memorize as much of the textbook chapter as possible.

The issue of student knowledge about the what, how, when, and why of learning strategies is only one theoretical issue in current research on students' learning strategies. Another issue concerns the role of students' metacognition. Although there is considerable theoretical confusion and disagreement about the definition and status of the construct of metacognition (Brown, 1987; Brown, Bransford, Ferrara, and Campione, 1983), metacognition generally refers to students' awareness and knowledge about cognition as well as their control and self-regulation of cognition (Brown, Bransford, Ferrara, and Campione, 1983). Accordingly, besides students' declarative, procedural, and conditional knowledge about strategies for learning (metacognitive knowledge), current research has focused on how students control their use of learning strategies through planning, monitoring, and self-regulation activities (Corno, 1986; Corno and Mandinach, 1983; Weinstein and Mayer, 1986). For example, planning activities include setting goals for studying, skimming, generating questions before reading the text, and doing a task analysis of the problem (McKeachie, Pintrich, Lin, and Smith, 1986; Weinstein and Mayer, 1986). All these activities are assumed to help the learners plan their use of other cognitive strategies as well as prime, or activate, relevant prior knowledge. Monitoring and regulating activities include tracking of attention as one reads a text, self-testing for comprehension of the material, reviewing material if comprehension is lacking, and rereading if a passage is particularly difficult (McKeachie, Pintrich, Lin, and Smith, 1986; Weinstein and Mayer, 1986). The recent research clearly shows that students who engage in these types of metacognitive activities achieve at higher levels than students who do not control and regulate their cognition (Brown, 1987; Jacobs and Paris, 1987; Pressley, 1986).

These positive results suggest that, although cognitive and developmental researchers may argue over the theoretical status and usefulness of the construct of metacognition, it may be more important to consider the practical issue of how to teach students both the knowledge about strategies as well as how to control and regulate their cognition. There have been a variety of programs designed to teach students learning strategies and study skills over the years (see Kulik, Kulik, and Shwalb, 1983). However, many of these programs have not been based on strong theoretical frameworks about how students process information (Weinstein and Underwood, 1985). More recently, programs have been developed that are based on the research findings in cognitive psychology and attempt to teach students a variety of cognitive and metacognitive skills. For example, Dansereau (1985) has developed a program called MURDER that provides students with specific methods to improve their comprehension of text materials; it includes such methods as selecting the main ideas and then diagramming the relationships among the main ideas. Weinstein and her colleagues at the University of Texas (Weinstein and Underwood, 1985) have developed a semester-long college course designed to teach students basic cognitive strategies, such as how to summarize readings for the main ideas, note-taking strategies, metacognitive strategies like planning and goal setting, as well as such resource management strategies as management of time and study environment. At the University of Michigan, Bill McKeachie has developed a course to teach students general learning strategies (McKeachie, Pintrich, and Lin, 1985; Pintrich, McKeachie, and Lin, 1986). One unique feature of the course is that it attempts to teach students not only the declarative and procedural knowledge about learning strategies but also conditional knowledge. In this "Learning to Learn" course students are taught about the cognitive psychology underlying the learning strategies with the assumption that this knowledge about why the strategies work will facilitate students' use of appropriate strategies in different situations.

Currently, this issue of transfer, or how to get students to use the learning strategies taught to them in one course in a different course, is one of the most important research and practical problems facing the field of student learning. At the heart of this transfer issue is the question about the domain-specificity or generalizability of cognitive strategies. As Campione and Armbruster (1985) point out, there are two general positions in this debate, one group of researchers stresses the need for instruction in specific task or knowledge-based strategies (Levin, 1986), while other researchers emphasize the importance of learning general cognitive strategies (Weinstein and Mayer, 1986). Most of the learning strategy programs described above as well as all general study skills courses would be placed on the general cognitive side of this debate. Although these general programs can be effective, recent research at the University of Michigan (Doljanac, 1987; Pintrich, 1987b) has shown that different learning strategies may be differentially effective depending on the type of course (English, biology, or sociology) as well as the type of assignment or task involved in the course (multiple-choice test, essay exam, paper, lab assignment). The results of these studies of actual college students in actual courses, along with the results from more experimental studies (see Weinstein and Mayer, 1986), suggest that general learning strategy instructional programs may need to stress the conditional knowledge aspect of learning strategies over the declarative and procedural aspects. Accordingly, it is important to teach students not only about the strategies and how to employ them but also about when—that is, for what kinds of tasks—and why they may want to employ them. A focus on conditional knowledge in these general learning strategy courses should foster both student metacognitive awareness of strategies and student metacognition in terms of self-regulation and control of cognition.

Teaching students about the different types of learning strategies that are available, thereby facilitating metacognitive awareness, is the traditional function of study skills courses. Teaching students about self-regulation is easier than fostering actual self-regulation. Although learning strategy instructional programs must be designed for transfer, student motivational factors also play a role in transfer of learning strategies. In many of the cognitive models of student learning, motivational aspects of students are not considered or they are poorly conceptualized. However, with recent cognitive reformulations of motivation theory, there are a number of researchers who are attempting to link motivation and cognition to obtain a better description of student learning (McKeachie, Pintrich, Lin, and Smith, 1986; Paris and Oka, 1986; Pintrich, Cross,

Kozma, and McKeachie, 1986; Weinert and Kluwe, 1987). This new line of research on the interactions of motivation and cognition seems to show that students' motivational patterns are inextricably linked to their use of cognitive and metacognitive strategies. For example, Pintrich (1987a) has shown that such motivational characteristics as expectancy for success (the belief that one can succeed at a task) and task value (students' intrinsic interest in and belief about the importance of a task) are positively related to students' use of basic cognitive learning strategies as well as their use of metacognitive strategies.

Specifically, Pintrich (1987a) found that college students could be clustered into five general types of students depending on their actual grades in the course, their motivational characteristics, and their use of cognitive and metacognitive strategies (or self-regulation). The first group of students was comprised of the excellent students. These were students who received an *A* in the course and were high in motivation and self-regulation. The second group of students were the poor students who were low in motivation, did not report much self-regulation, and received grades below a *C* for the course. The other three groups of students were average in terms of their performance (*B*'s or *C*'s) but showed different motivational and cognitive patterns. The third group of students were low in the use of cognitive and metacognitive strategies but high in motivation. These students were motivated to do well but did not seem to use the cognitive and self-regulation strategies that would improve their performance. These students would appear to be the ones who would benefit most from a learning strategy training program. The fourth group consisted of students who used appropriate cognitive and metacognitive strategies but did not believe the course was interesting or valuable (one aspect of student motivation), although they were confident of their ability to do the work (a second aspect of motivation). These students essentially did not believe that the course work was that important to them and did not do as well as they might have, given their cognitive skills. The last group of students also used appropriate cognitive and metacognitive strategies but did not believe that they were capable of doing the work, even though they thought the course was important. These students did not feel confident in their skills and did not perform up to their capabilities.

Although these results need to be replicated, they shed some light on the dynamic interplay of motivation and cognition in the setting of the college classroom and suggest that motivational and cognitive components of student learning do not operate in isolation from one another but rather support and complement one another. Students can be skilled in the use of cognitive and self-regulating strategies, but motivational beliefs influence how these skills are used in different courses. This type of research on the relationships between student motivation and cognition promises to be a fruitful one for future research and should result in a more complete picture of the college student learner that integrates both motivational and cognitive aspects of student learning.

In summary, the research on student learning strategies provides an excellent description of the types of cognitive and metacognitive strategies that influence student learning in the college classroom. By focusing on the specific cognitive processes students actually use when trying to learn, remember, and understand course material, these newer cognitive models are more relevant to the actual tasks of teaching and learning and represent improvements over other models of student learning that stress personality variables or cognitive style variables, such as independence-dependence, reflectivity-impulsivity. Finally, this research suggests that instructors in all discipline areas, not just instructors in study skills courses, may want to think about how to teach students to use appropriate learning strategies in order to facilitate student learning in their courses.

Research on Students' Critical Thinking

Currently, almost all educators from the elementary level on through to the postsecondary level have become interested in how to teach students higher-order thinking skills, such as critical thinking, problem solving, and reasoning skills. There are a number of recent books available on the topic that describe a variety of different programs to teach students higher-order thinking skills (Baron and Sternberg, 1987; Brookfield, 1987; Chipman, Segal, and Glaser, 1985; Meyers, 1986; Nickerson, Perkins, and Smith, 1985; Segal, Chipman, and Glaser, 1985). There are too many different programs to summarize them all in this paper, but a few general comments may be made about the programs and their relevance to college teaching and learning. First, even a cursory glance at the content of these different programs reveals that there are a multitude of terms, constructs, definitions, and models of critical thinking and problem solving. Although it is beyond the scope of this chapter to clarify the theoretical confusion surrounding the topic of critical thinking, it is important to note that both researchers and practitioners have different conceptualizations of critical thinking and different models for teaching critical thinking. Secondly, many of these programs are designed to be used by the teacher as a supplement or as an addition to the regular curriculum. Finally, these general supplementary or "add-on" programs may involve skills that are more applicable at the elementary or secondary levels than at the postsecondary level. Accordingly, before college faculty attempt to utilize these programs for their own courses, they need to examine the relevance of the content, the definition and model of critical thinking proposed, and the instructional methods suggested for use by the program.

Another consideration relevant to any application of this work at the postsecondary level is the research support for the theoretical model underlying the program and the empirical evidence for the effectiveness of the program. Some of the programs may be based on theoretical models that do not have strong research support in the current cognitive psychology literature. In addition, many of the programs present very little research or evaluation data regarding the effectiveness of the program for teaching higher-order skills. In addition, these programs often do not empirically examine the relative effectiveness of different components of their program. For example, these programs often provide a variety of activities, tasks, and problems that can be used to foster students' critical thinking, but it is not clear if all the activities and tasks are equally necessary or important for teaching critical thinking. As Levin (1986) has noted, there is a need for the componential analysis of the different skills involved in teaching higher-order skills as well as an evaluation of the different instructional practices that comprise these programs (Glaser, 1984). In summary, the research on the different formal programs for teaching critical thinking may provide useful background information for college faculty interested in teaching critical thinking, but it may not provide information that can be applied directly to the college classroom.

Besides the research on formal programs for critical thinking, there has been a great deal of research on the impact of college on students' critical thinking. In an attempt to summarize the research on the college classroom and students' critical thinking, McMillan (1986) concluded, "The results failed to support the use of specific instructional or course conditions to enhance critical thinking but did support the conclusion that college in general appears to improve critical thinking." This conclusion parallels research on developmental trends in college students' thinking that shows that students' level of cognitive development or "stage" of thinking increases over the college years (Commons, Richards, and Armon, 1984; Mines and Kitchener, 1986; Perry, 1970). Although this trend in students' thinking is positive, from an instructional psychology point of view (Pintrich, Cross, Kozma, and McKeachie, 1986), it does not really provide a framework for analyzing the college classroom and the types of instructional strategies and activities faculty members might use if they want to take a more active role in facilitating students' thinking. For example, McKeachie, Pintrich, Lin, and Smith (1986), in a more positive review of the college teaching and critical thinking literature, suggested that three aspects of instruction make a difference: (1) student discussion, (2) explicit emphasis on problem-solving procedures and methods, and (3) verbalization and modeling of thinking strategies to encourage the development of metacognition.

For example, the research on students' critical thinking at Alverno College (Loacker, Cromwell, Fey, and Rutherford, 1984; Mentkowski and Strait, 1983) suggests that direct instruction in critical thinking results in student growth. The program at Alverno is important in several respects. First, it represents the development of a "local" model of critical thinking that then serves to guide instruction and assessment. The development of a local model of critical thinking can be applied not just at the institutional level, but at the individual course level by the instructor. For example, a biology instructor might decide that critical thinking in her course involves scientific reasoning and problem solving and design her instruction to reflect this emphasis (the use of experiments, modeling of data collection and analysis procedures). In addition, this biology instructor could then use assessment strategies that match the goals and instructional strategies (laboratory assignments). In contrast, an English instructor might assume that critical thinking in a literature class should involve thematic analysis of the novels and short stories assigned as readings. In this example, the instructor would try to facilitate critical thinking by demonstrating how to perform a thematic analysis of a text and by providing assignments that require students to perform their own thematic analyses. The idea that there may be discipline or subject matter differences in what constitutes critical thinking and how to teach it is in line with the models of student thinking that emphasize the importance of the students' knowledge base as discussed above (see also Glaser, 1984). In addition, this notion of a "local" model of critical thinking allows faculty the freedom to decide for themselves what skills they want to consider as critical thinking and then to design their courses in such a way to foster those skills.

The work at Alverno also highlights the importance of directly teaching critical thinking skills through modeling and verbalization of the different strategies actually used by faculty as they think critically about the course content. In addition, the students must have the opportunity to practice these skills in different situations and tasks. This emphasis on direct instruction by the teacher parallels work at the elementary and secondary levels on the teaching of reading comprehension skills (Paris, Cross, and Lipson, 1984) and math problem-solving strategies (Pressley, 1986) as well as other content areas (see review by Pintrich, McKeachie, and Lin, 1986). The important implication of this research for teaching is that it suggests that many students will not intuitively learn critical thinking or problem-solving skills by merely attending college. The college experience and the courses offered must be explicitly designed and taught in such a way as to facilitate student learning of these skills.

Although there are certain limitations on course format (for example, active student discussion of course material may be difficult in a lecture course with an enrollment of two hundred), the recent research on academic tasks (Doyle, 1983) suggests some ways in which faculty members may change their course assignments to encourage more critical thinking. The notion of academic tasks assumes that the assignments students are asked to complete as course requirements guide and organize students' information processing (Brown, Bransford, Ferrara, and Campione, 1983; Doyle, 1983). For example, multiple-choice tests that stress knowledge of factual information may encourage students to use a different type of cognitive learning strategy than an essay exam that stresses application of the material to a new situation (rote rehearsal strategies versus analogical thinking). Research on "surface" orientations to learning (a focus on memorization of facts) versus a "deep" orientation (a focus on understanding and comprehension) has demonstrated that the nature of the task or assessment system greatly influences students' adoption of a learning orientation (Entwistle and Ramsden, 1983; Ramsden, 1985). Accordingly, if students can receive good grades on an exam or assignment by employing a surface orientation focused on memorization of facts, then they will tend to use cognitive strategies that may not result in as much deep processing and comprehension of the course material. Furthermore, this problem is compounded by findings suggesting that many unversity exams only focus on the lower cognitive levels of information processing, such as recall and recognition of course material, and not the higher levels of analysis, synthesis, or evaluation (Crooks and Collins, 1986).

Although there has not been a great deal of research on the nature of academic tasks and assignments at the college level and their interactions with student learning and thinking, this academic task perspective promises to be an important one for both theory and practice. Better descriptions of how actual college course assignments influence student learning and thinking will add "real world" validity to the many experimental studies of cognition and should result in refinements in our theories about the nature of student learning in the college classroom. In addition, the focus on academic tasks and assignments provides a very practical "tool" that can be used for instructional improvement. Faculty members may not have control over the size and format of their classes, or the types of students that attend their classes (students with varying levels of content knowledge, differential skill in the use of learning strategies, or differential motivational patterns), but they generally have control over the types of assignments in their courses. If the academic task notion is valid and tasks do guide the ways students process the course material, then changing the types of tasks assigned can result in changes in the way students come to learn and think about the course material.

Conclusion

The theoretical models and empirical results that are emerging from the current research on students' knowledge, learning strategies, and critical thinking provide excellent descriptions of how college students come to learn, remember, and understand course material. These descriptions of the cognitive psychology of the learner, although they may be rather sophisticated at times, represent a substantial improvement over earlier models of student learning that did not adequately capture the complexity of the learning process. Of course, these current models do not provide all the answers to questions about student learning and cognition in the college classroom and more research is always needed. Nevertheless, this research does represent an advance in our understanding of student learning and does have implications for instruction. As McKeachie, Pintrich, Lin, and Smith (1986), have pointed out, this research may not result in the discovery of new teaching strategies, or the one "best" method of instruction, or a magic elixir for fostering student learning and motivation, but it can help college faculty conceptualize teaching and learning in new ways. These new conceptualizations or beliefs about teaching and learning can then be used by faculty members as the knowledge base to draw upon as they attempt to interact effectively with different students in different instructional settings.

References

Anderson, J. R. *Cognitive Psychology and Its Implications.* New York: Freeman, 1985.

Baron, J., and Sternberg, R. *Teaching Thinking Skills.* New York: Freeman, 1987.

Bok, D. *Higher Learning.* Cambridge, Mass.: Harvard University Press, 1986.

Boyer, E. *College: The Undergraduate Experience in America.* New York: Harper & Row, 1987.

Bransford, J. D., Sherwood, R., Vye, N., and Rieser, J. "Teaching Thinking and Problem Solving: Research Foundations." *American Psychologist,* 1986, *41,* 1078–1089.

Brookfield, S. *Developing Critical Thinkers: Challenging Adults to Explore Alternative Ways of Thinking and Acting.* San Francisco: Jossey-Bass, 1987.

Brown, A. "Metacognition, Executive Control, Self-Regulation, and Other More Mysterious Mechanisms." In F. Weinert and R. Kluwe (eds.), *Metacognition, Motivation, and Understanding.* Hillsdale, N.J.: Erlbaum, 1987.

Brown, A. L., Bransford, J. D., Ferrara, R. A., and Campione, J. C. "Learning, Remembering, and Understanding." In P. H. Mussen (ed.), *Handbook of Child Psychology.* Vol. 3. New York: Wiley, 1983.

Campione, J. C., and Armbruster, B. B. "Acquiring Information from Texts: An Analysis of Four Approaches." In J. W. Segal, S. F. Chipman, and E. R. Glaser (eds.), *Thinking and Learning Skills.* Vol. 1. Hillsdale, N. J.: Erlbaum, 1985.

Cantor, N., and Kihlstrom, J. *Personality and Social Intelligence.* Englewood Cliffs, N.J.: Prentice-Hall, 1987.

Chipman, S., Segal, J., and Glaser, R. *Thinking and Learning Skills: Research Issues.* Vol. 2. Hillsdale, N.J.: Erlbaum, 1985.

Commons, M., Richards, F., and Armon, C. *Beyond Formal Operations: Late Adolescent and Adult Cognitive Development.* New York: Praeger, 1984.

Corno, L. *Self-Regulated Learning and Classroom Teaching.* Paper presented at the American Educational Research Association convention, San Francisco, 1986.

Corno, L., and Mandinach, E. "The Role of Cognitive Engagement in Classroom Learning and Motivation." *Educational Psychologist,* 1983, *18,* 88–100.

Corno, L., and Snow, R. "Adapting Teaching to Individual Differences Among Learners." In M. Wittrock (ed.), *Handbook of Research on Teaching.* New York: Macmillan, 1986.

Crooks, T., and Collins, E. "What Do First Year University Examinations Assess?" *New Zealand Journal of Educational Studies,* 1986, *21* (2), 123–132.

Dansereau, D. "Learning Strategy Research." In J. Segal, S. Chipman, and R. Glaser (eds.), *Thinking and Learning Skills: Relating Instruction to Research.* Vol. 1. Hillsdale, N.J.: Erlbaum, 1985.

Doljanac, R. *The Role of Learning Strategies in the College Classroom.* Paper presented at the American Psychological Association convention, New York, 1987.

Doyle, W. "Academic Work." *Review of Educational Research,* 1983, *53,* 159–199.

Entwistle, N. J., and Ramsden, P. *Understanding Student Learning.* London: Croom Helm, 1983.

Gagne, E. *The Cognitive Psychology of School Learning.* Boston: Little, Brown, 1985.

Glaser, R. "Education and Thinking: The Role of Knowledge." *American Psychologist,* 1984, *39,* 93–104.

Jacobs, J., and Paris, S. "Children's Metacognition About Reading: Issues in Definition, Measurement, and Instruction." *Educational Psychologist,* 1987, *22,* 255–278.

Kulik, C. L., Kulik, J. A., and Shwalb, B. J. "College Programs for High-Risk and Disadvantaged Students: A Meta-Analysis of Findings." *Review of Educational Research,* 1983, *53,* 397–414.

Levin, J. R. "Four Cognitive Principles of Learning-Strategy Instruction." *Educational Psychologist,* 1986, *21* (1 and 2), 3–17.

Loacker, G., Cromwell, L., Fey, J., and Rutherford, D. *Analysis and Communication at Alverno: An Approach to Critical Thinking.* Milwaukee, Wis.: Alverno Productions, 1984.

McKeachie, W. J. (ed.). *Learning, Cognition, and College Teaching.* New Directions for Teaching and Learning, no. 2. San Francisco: Jossey-Bass, 1980.

McKeachie, W. J., Pintrich, P. R., and Lin, Y. G. "Teaching and Learning Strategies." *Educational Psychologist,* 1985, *20* (3), 153–160.

McKeachie, W. J., Pintrich, P. R., Lin, Y. G., and Smith, D. *Teaching and Learning in the College Classroom: A Review of the Research Literature.* Ann Arbor: National Center for Research to Improve Postsecondary Teaching and Learning, University of Michigan, 1986.

McMillan, J. *Enhancing College Students' Critical Thinking: A Review of Studies.* Paper presented at the American Educational Research Association convention, San Francisco, 1986.

Mentkowski, M., and Strait, M. J. *A Longitudinal Study of Student Change in Cognitive Development, Learning Styles, and Generic Abilities in an Outcome-Centered Liberal Arts Curriculum.* Milwaukee, Wis.: Alverno Productions, 1983. (ED 239 562)

85

Meyers, C. *Teaching Students to Think Critically: A Guide for Faculty in All Disciplines.* San Francisco: Jossey-Bass, 1986.

Mines, R., and Kitchener, K. *Adult Cognitive Development: Methods and Models.* New York: Praeger, 1986.

National Institute of Education (NIE) Study Group. *Involvement in Learning: Realizing the Potential of American Higher Education.* Washington, D.C.: U.S. Government Printing Office, 1984.

Naveh-Benjamin, M., and Lin, Y. G. *Development of Cognitive Structures in University Courses and Their Relations to Students' Study Skills, Anxiety, and Motivation.* Paper presented at the American Psychological Association convention, New York, 1987.

Naveh-Benjamin, M., McKeachie, W. J., Lin, Y. G., and Tucker, D. "Inferring Students' Cognitive Structure and Their Development Using the 'Ordered-Tree Technique.' " *Journal of Educational Psychology,* 1986, *78,* 130-140.

Nickerson, R., Perkins, D., and Smith, E. *The Teaching of Thinking.* Hillsdale, N.J.: Erlbaum, 1985.

Paris, S., Cross, D., and Lipson, M. "Informed Strategies for Learning: A Program to Improve Children's Reading Awareness and Comprehension." *Journal of Educational Psychology,* 1984, *76,* 1239-1252.

Paris, S., Lipson, M., and Wixson, K. "Becoming a Strategic Reader." *Contemporary Educational Psychology,* 1983, *8,* 293-316.

Paris, S., and Oka, E. "Children's Reading Strategies, Metacognition, and Motivation." *Developmental Review,* 1986, *6,* 25-56.

Perry, W. *Forms of Intellectual and Ethical Development in the College Years: A Scheme.* New York: Holt, Rinehart, and Winston, 1970.

Pintrich, P. R. *Motivated Learning Strategies in the College Classroom.* Paper presented at the American Educational Research Association convention, Washington, D.C., 1987a.

Pintrich, P. R. *The Role of Critical Thinking and Problem Solving in the College Classroom.* Paper presented at the American Psychological Association convention, New York, 1987b.

Pintrich, P. R., Cross, D., Kozma, R., and McKeachie, W. J. "Instructional Psychology." *Annual Review of Psychology,* 1986, *37,* 611-651.

Pintrich, P. R., McKeachie, W., and Lin, Y. G. "Teaching a Learning to Learn Class." *Teaching of Psychology,* 1986, *14,* 81-86.

Pressley, M. "The Relevance of the Good Strategy Used Model to the Teaching of Mathematics." *Educational Psychologist,* 1986, *21,* 139-161.

Ramsden, P. "Student Learning Research: Retrospect and Prospect." *Higher Education Research and Development,* 1985, *4,* 51-69.

Schunk, D. H. "Self-Efficacy and Classroom Learning." *Psychology in the Schools,* 1985, *22,* 208-223.

Segal, J., Chipman, S., and Glaser, R. (eds.). *Thinking and Learning Skills: Relating Instruction to Research.* Vol. 1. Hillsdale, N.J.: Erlbaum, 1985.

Shulman, L. S. "Paradigms and Research Programs in the Study of Teaching: A Contemporary Perspective." In M. Wittrock (ed.), *The Handbook of Research on Teaching.* New York: Macmillan, 1986.

Snow, R. E., and Peterson, P. L. "Recognizing Differences in Student Aptitudes." In W. J. McKeachie (ed.), *Learning, Cognition, and College Teaching.* New Directions for Teaching and Learning, no. 2. San Francisco: Jossey-Bass, 1980.

Weinert, F., and Kluwe, R. *Metacognition, Motivation, and Understanding.* Hillsdale, N.J.: Erlbaum, 1987.

Weinstein, C., and Mayer, R. "The Teaching of Learning Strategies." In

M. Wittrock (ed.), *Handbook of Research on Teaching*. New York: Macmillan, 1986.

Weinstein, C., and Underwood, V. "Learning Strategies: The How of Learning." In J. Segal, S. Chipman, and R. Glaser (eds.), *Thinking and Learning Skills: Relating Instruction to Research*. Vol. 1. Hillsdale, N.J.: Erlbaum, 1985.

Young, R. *A Critical Look at the Research on Motivation, Learning Strategies, and Critical Thinking*. Paper presented at the American Psychological Association convention, New York, 1987.

Paul R. Pintrich is assistant professor of education in the School of Education and assistant research scientist with the National Center for Research to Improve Postsecondary Teaching and Learning at the University of Michigan.

The quality of teaching depends greatly on the attention faculty give to it amidst conflicting claims on their time and energies.

The Contexts of College Teaching, Past and Future

Kenneth E. Eble

Almost ten years ago, I began editing this series, *New Directions for Teaching and Learning*. Ten years before that I was midway in a two-year effort directing the Project to Improve College Teaching. Ten years before that I was fairly new to the teaching profession and asking an eminent Harvard professor who had just delivered a scholarly address, "How does a college teacher handle all the things that are expected: teaching and research and serving on committees and keeping up with one's field and publishing and all the rest?"

His answer was that if you were the right stuff, you didn't worry about such things. He did not use the term "the right stuff"—this was before "the right stuff" put us on the moon—but whatever his terms, I knew I was being put down. I also sensed he was wrong. A lifetime by now of professing and working with thousands of professors makes me certain he was wrong. Being the right stuff is not sufficient to maintain teaching at a decent level within the many and diverse institutions that purport to educate students at a higher level.

College and university teaching has contexts that are ignored to the denigration of teaching and that college teachers during much of their careers must cope with in order to survive. Some of these are the contexts that bothered me as a novice professor—those many demands on

R. E. Young, K. E. Eble (eds.). *College Teaching and Learning: Preparing for New Commitments.*
New Directions for Teaching and Learning, no. 33. San Francisco: Jossey-Bass, Spring 1988.

a professor's time that teaching often gets done in spite of. Others are personal and civic contexts that affect any occupation. The contexts I choose to explore here are some of those that are important to teaching and learning. Specific aspects of each have appeared as topics in this series and as subjects for chronic debate among college faculties.

The four I choose to discuss—and there are others of equal importance—are research and publishing, kinds of students, what is known about teaching, and presence or absence of learning communities.

Research and Publishing

The first context is that of scholarship, the necessary carrying on of research and publishing that causes so much anguish in decisions about retention, promotion, and tenure. It is at the heart of the college and university reward system, and during my two decades of systematically trying to improve college teaching faculty have cited changing the reward system as the most needed step toward improvement. Three observations that may be reasonably up-to-date are that (1) the preoccupation with research has become pretty much a fetish, (2) faculties have increasingly become separated into research and teaching faculties, and (3) the central core disciplines of the liberal arts have been further pulled away from teaching by an overfondness for theory.

Fetish with Research. As to research being a fetish, I use the term in the sense of its dictionary definition: "that which elicits unquestioning reverence, respect or devotion," and "that which, though not of a sexual nature causes an erotic response or fixation." You show me your research and I'll show you mine.

Few academic voices are ever raised about the obsessive nature of this behavior or even about the glut of research. Jacques Barzun is a recent exception, citing the triviality of much scholarship and making this common-sense observation: "To suppose that every owner of a Ph.D. can carry on valuable research while also teaching, and find time to write it up in publishable form, is contrary to fact" (1987, p. 2).

Still, the flood pours forth and no responsible confrontation of the research fetish is likely to come from the universities themselves. The present incoming generation of teachers is under more personal and institutional pressure to do research than those they are replacing. Within most of the traditional liberal arts disciplines young faculty are, in part because of a tight academic job market, wed to research and publishing, adhering to demands of the discipline, and keeping on the right side of individuals and institutions that might keep them employed.

In addition, the prominence of science and technology since World War II has shaped pursuits and practices for almost all other disciplines, much as the research university has exerted a powerful influence on all other institutions in the academic hierarchy. It is hard to resist success, and research has had a long run of practical success. For faculty, research has been a way of escaping teaching as well as pursuing knowledge. Most recent Ph.D.'s still have to teach, and many are under some scrutiny to teach well.

Teaching and Research Faculties. The strains between doing specialized scholarship and teaching are greater now than in the past. Within most of our large institutions, we now have even more than in the past clearly identifiable but not often formally acknowledged teaching and research faculties. The identifying characteristics are size of teaching load, level of course taught, amount of outside grant funding, commitment to service or broadly educational functions, and ratio of graduate to undergraduate degrees conferred. Most science and engineering faculties fall into the research category; most of the liberal arts disciplines into the teaching one. To some degree these distinctions match those that separate graduate from undergraduate faculties.

But despite the obvious existence of a group of faculty who teach a lot and those who do not, higher education has resisted actual designations of separate faculties. A partial recognition of the importance of an undergraduate teaching faculty lies in the development of an undergraduate dean as the counterpart of the graduate dean. The rank of lecturer within the University of California system also serves to identify teaching faculty, though in an inadequate way. The reasons for the prevailing pattern of a single faculty are many. Within even the research university, many faculty members still want to teach—some. Public universities in particular may be sensitive to the fact that the public still believes that teaching is what college and university faculty are paid to do. And on the part of those consigned to or choosing the teaching faculty, actual separation of faculties might only be a confirming of secondary status.

Consequently, a designated teaching faculty is not as much in evidence as a loose corps of faculty at virtually every four-year college and university who are both good teachers and who maintain the institution's active and visible interest in teaching. Such groups vary in strength and number from institution to institution but few, except perhaps at small liberal arts colleges, comprise a majority of the faculty. The teaching corps at most colleges includes most but not all of the stellar teachers and some but not many of those whose reputations rest on published research.

This teaching corps feels its sense of minority status but has reasons to both value and lament it. It is from this corps that presidents draw stellar examples to convince a portion of the supporting constituency that undergraduate education is an institutional priority. That corps includes faculty who find great satisfaction from working more closely with students (and likely with more students). Such a corps may maintain some semblance of collegiality in shared curricula, team-taught courses, in a common interest in keeping undergraduate education vital. Some such explanations must be offered to explain the persistence of such a corps even in the face of powerful internal and external forces moving in opposite directions.

Nationally such a teaching faculty also exists in the form of those organizations within disciplinary associations devoted to teaching. They are to be found in engineering as in English, in political science as in mathematics. Most of them have long histories; most occupy a secondary status as compared with the sheltering organization.

While I think such a teaching corps exists in every institution, two anomalies are worth noting. The corps of faculty committed to and gaining great satisfaction from teaching is and should be large in liberal arts colleges. Paradoxically, that corps diminishes as an institution rises in prestige, for a more highly selected faculty and the need for wide visibility places considerable emphasis upon visible productivity. While a research faculty may not exist as it does at a major university, semblances of it do exist, affect the reward system, and eventuate in another part of the faculty carrying the main responsibility for maintaining the level of teaching that such colleges lead parents and students to expect. The second peculiarity is more of the past than the present—that is, the presence of some of the most distinguished scholars among the most compelling undergraduate teachers. I think it is becoming more difficult to generate stories of having a Polykarp Kusch or a Linus Pauling as one's freshman teacher, though such presences were always more uncommon than common in the lower-division experiences of most college students.

Fascination with Theory. There is, I think, a secondary effect of the preoccupation with research, and that is the current fascination with theory in many of the disciplines that form the central core of undergraduate work. This is to be easily explained as one more evidence of the higher level of education imposing its practices on the lower. But I will use the single example of my own field—English—to extend speculations about other causes. English has existed for much of its history as a broad field of study; however, its practices at the highest levels were highly specialized. The reasons are largely practical: reading and writing have been fundamental requirements for college success. The number of philologists or linguists or semioticians required within a college faculty will always be exceeded by the number of teachers of reading and writing. As higher education expanded, English grew away from its theoretical scholarly base and developed into an eclectic discipline sheltering great numbers of people willing to engage in basic instruction.

For most of this century, English departments carried out these service functions even if often as the price to be paid for engaging in more desirable scholarly activities. With the increasing pressures for jobs and the increasing attractiveness of prerogatives enjoyed by a research faculty, a drift away from service functions was inevitable.

It is not accidental that the preoccupation with theoretical literary criticism appears at a time when English is most threatened by both a loss of majors and the possibility of its becoming more of a service department than it is. Theory alone seems to provide the basis for the kind of research that will convince a supporting constituency that valuable, if little understood (and the less understood the better), work needs to be done. Speech long ago escaped into communication where a bristling theoretical orientation protects a faculty from a flood of students whose principal interest is not theory at all but getting one of those up-front jobs in the media.

The attraction of theory-laden scholarship may also be seen in the way in which newly emerged but still insecure disciplines have taken to it. Within English, feminist scholarship has already committed more offenses against the common tongue than the new criticism was able to commit in decades. And it is sad to see programs in minority literature and culture going the way of the established disciplines, buying into the very cultural patterns they might better oppose.

As all this relates to the scholarship context for college teaching, the difficulties for young faculty of keeping up with the discipline and producing theory-ridden research will continue to increase. Where there is no counter within an institution, more and more teaching will move to the faculty's immediate special interests and away from broad educational aims. The divisions between the unrecognized "teaching" and "research" faculties will grow and coherence in undergraduate education, seemingly much sought after currently, will remain an unrealized but vaguely upheld goal.

There is much more to be said about the relationship between teaching and research, seldom honestly faced at any period of American higher education. The simplest thing to be said is that the name "research university" has only within two decades become the accepted term to describe the "flagship institutions" (an even more recent term) that dominate American higher education. All the public relations pronouncements to the contrary cannot disguise the fact that teaching in such institutions plays a secondary role.

Students

The second broad context for teaching is the students. A fundamental reality of all teaching is that teachers probably prefer to teach students most like themselves. College and university faculty today may find this a source of conflict. Both the long-term movement of American higher education and the growth of the sixties and seventies have diversi-

92

fied student populations in almost every kind of institution. Acceptance of that fact by faculty is only an acknowledgment of reality. But at the same time, the values and preferences of the faculty in many ways run counter to that diversity. The community college system seems to offer, for four-year college faculty, a convenient place to process or screen out less desirable students. Remedial instruction continues to fall to faculty least able to protect themselves from it. For an individual faculty member, the way out from, say, an open-admission urban university is to publish the kinds of things that will be attractive to more selective institutions. Or, as an alternative, to become a successful administrator of "developmental," that is, remedial programs so that the teaching falls to others.

There is nothing new or startling about the desire to escape drudgery in any occupation. Higher education is shot through with indefensible practices rooted in such individual and collective desires. With less mobility, with lessened sense of public responsibility, with increasing financial pressures on institutions, a great portion of faculty will be teaching great numbers of students somewhat down the scale from what that faculty member would most like.

Some faculty will not be greatly affected. They have accepted student ignorance, human ignorance, as the necessary condition on which their existence as teachers depends. And some find the greatest of satisfactions in assisting students who have furthest to go. But both despite and because of the steady expansion of American higher education, the need to adjust faculty perspectives will become more pressing and will affect teaching adversely where it does not get made or gets made grudgingly.

With respect to that growing minority population that should be expected to contribute a proportionate share of college students, current trends are discouraging. Because of the waning energies toward civil rights and for other causes as well, black, Hispanic, Asian, and Native American enrollments in undergraduate colleges have not increased as expected. The numbers of blacks and Hispanics applying to graduate schools with prospects of becoming college professors have dropped sharply. The situation right now reflects both the condition I have described—a tendency for teachers to prefer teaching those like themselves—and a symptom of deeper ill—the exclusion of minority groups from full participation in American society.

Learning About Teaching and Learning

The third context is the one that provoked and supports these sourcebooks: what the faculty know and put into practice about teaching and learning. The volumes in this series are evidence that we know something. The small size of audience they reach is an indicator of how little of what we know is likely to get into practice.

The second volume in this series was on cognitive psychology and what it was finding out about how people learn. One of the most widely publicized recent books on education is E. D. Hirsch's *Cultural Literacy*, which draws heavily upon cognitive theory with respect to reading and writing. The evidence that reading depends heavily on acquiring "schemata" does appear to be an advancement in knowledge. Reasonable ways of developing such schemata may be possible. At the same time, it is no new knowledge that contexts are important to learning, that we abstract and aggregate in order to understand, that we need to know things as well as acquire skills.

Outside the field of education and educational psychology, college faculty do have resistance to research into pedagogy. Derek Bok (1986) in *Higher Learning* writes: "Apprehensive about educational research and skeptical of its validity, faculties give the work such a low priority and status that their skepticism becomes self-fulfilling" (p. 67). But good teachers acquire a good deal through experience, discussion with colleagues, and even their own patient inquiries into how students learn. While I have spent much of my life deploring the low priority given to specific preparation for college teaching and to the resistance later on to learning about teaching, I see at least one positive aspect. That is that college and university faculty are also resistant to the panaceas that regularly come into public school education, usually based on research that greatly simplifies the complex matters of teaching at any level. Behavioral objectives have come and gone, but mastery learning and performance-based education are still with us; the mention of Hirsch's book, itself a simplistic rendering of research evidence, indicates that "cultural literacy" will join "critical thinking" as a current catchword.

"Cultural literacy" runs somewhat counter to "critical thinking," both seeking to provide the one handle best designed to turn the educational machine to account. Each seems to reflect a political position, with cultural literacy appealing to the educational right, even though the nation has seldom had a chief executive less in command of fact and more adept at process. Critical thinking, as it actually is critical (and much of it is not), is either from the romantic left that Hirsch deplores or the more recent left that has now taken to thinking, since feeling alone did not manage to overturn the establishment.

Such movements and the books and articles that launch and support them at least raise the possibility that faculty are thinking about the actualities of how students learn. The growth of faculty development and school/college cooperation and collaboration are two other measures of an increased interest by college faculty in the hows of teaching and learning. Few of the many faculty development programs now going on do not give specific attention to developing teaching strategies and practices. The removal of some of the barriers between public schools and colleges may mean greater knowledgeability about a wider range of student learning.

Communities for Learning?

A fourth context for teaching—and there are far more contexts than these—is the presence or lack of presence of a community for learning. For almost twenty years now, I have observed little community in the large institutions that set the pattern for teaching in academia. I will use my own university as a representative example of a pattern of diminished community over this span. One index is the breaking up of a unified College of Letters and Science into three separate colleges. Another is the disappearance of university-wide forums for discussion of scholarly, educational, or public issues. Another is the disappearance of modest quarters for the faculty club, chiefly because few faculty used those facilities. Another is the increasingly separate languages of scholarship, not just in the sciences but in the humanities as well. Another is the waning of the sense of obligation to perform university committee work or to serve on the faculty senate. Another is the decline in attendance at commencement and other similar functions. Another is the increase in the number of personal computers and coffeepots. Another . . . but the list is already too long and is not intended as a piling up of hard evidence anyway.

It may be that a community of scholars signified by a collection of buildings in some "Athens of the Plains" is as anachronistic as a city "downtown." Reviving of community in higher education may be more difficult than reviving downtowns, if only because universities have not yet recognized the possibility of turning some decaying portion of the campus into an "Old Town." How might a public flock to see ancient professors working at manual typewriters, buy Greek-letter key and neck chains, and marvel at high-priced, high-fashion, educational antiquities?

The question may be whether there is still some segment of a university population resistant to the shopping-mall contours of the new campus community. Presidents have pretty much bought into this new design and are concerned chiefly with lining up two or three anchor establishments—the stadium, of course, but the indoor arenas as well, and the science and technology complex, and the wellness center—that will attract enough consumers in bulk to float an array of lesser tenants. Students will take what they find, and their community has never been the faculty's anyway. As long as someone provides videogames and keeps the change machine filled and the daytime soaps on the big-screen TV, there will be places for community. Alumni will gather wherever there is room to put a tailgate down and opportunity to verify that athletes are exerting themselves at some rate commensurate with what they are being paid.

That leaves the faculty, and among the faculty, those committed to teaching more than any other group. Much of research, like most of writing, is lonely work, in which friends, lovers, and family are intrusions, baneful in direct proportion to their numbers and the intensity of relationship. Much of teaching is social, demanding listeners and talkers and demonstraters and questioners, a marketplace even if its dimensions are only those of a classroom. Perhaps these factors, dwelt upon and extended, are the one source of optimism about community contexts favorable to teaching. Some students still seek out teachers, and some teachers still find teaching a community enterprise from the exciting beginning of a school year to its often exhausting end. Maybe those classroom communities are the best the current shape of American higher education can offer. And maybe the great numbers of still small colleges can attract students and retain faculty because communities, however modest and off the fast track they may be, do exist there, and therefore teaching and learning can find a necessary home.

References

Barzun, J. "Doing Research—Should the Sport Be Regulated?" *Columbia*, 1987, *12* (4), 1-5.
Bok, D. *Higher Learning*. Cambridge, Mass.: Harvard University Press, 1986.
Hirsch, E. D., Jr. *Cultural Literacy: What Every American Needs to Know*. Boston: Houghton Mifflin, 1987.

Kenneth E. Eble is professor of English, University of Utah, and consulting editor, New Directions for Teaching and Learning.

Index